Wide Awake
Poets of Los Angeles and Beyond

Edited by Suzanne Lummis

Pacific Coast Poetry Series
Founding Editor, Henry J. Morro

Wide Awake
Poets of Los Angeles and Beyond

Copyright © 2015 Pacific Coast Poetry Series
An imprint of Beyond Baroque Books
ISBN: 978-1-892184-03-0

Editor
Suzanne Lummis

Assistant Editor
Liz Camfiord

Cover Design
Joanne Minerbi

Cover Photo
Jupiter, Venus and the Moon above Los Angeles
By Dave Jurasevich

Beyond Baroque Literary Arts Center
Beyond Baroque Books
Pacific Coast Poetry Series

681 Venice Boulevard
Venice, CA, 90291

310-822-3006
www.beyondbaroque.org

This collection is dedicated to those we lost along the way, the Los Angeles poets Wanda Coleman and Bill Hickok, and to the poet whose teachings and writings touched so many in this region (and beyond), Philip Levine.

TABLE OF CONTENTS

* Regarding this idiosyncrasy in the order of poets, the editor felt this poem would flourish best in this context, so it has been separated from the other three of Mezey's poems.

INTRODUCTION

Against Dreaming

Our outer limits, which poets needed to live within to be considered for this particular publication, stretched south to Long Beach, east to Claremont, north to Ventura and west to the great Pacific, but in the public imagination, private one too, I suppose—sometimes—these far-flung cities and municipalities seem to gather themselves around a 502.7 square mile spread of humanity. The place has purchase on various types of fame and distinction, some good and not all of them exaggerated or misconstrued, but the most indisputable of these is this: No other city was founded with such a long, majestic name that then shrank to such tininess —from *El Pueblo de Nuestra Señora la Reina de los Ángeles del Río de Porciúncula** to—*L.A.*

Beat that, Other Cities.

We've given this collection a manageable name, *Wide Awake*, to counter those phrases and nicknames for the city that suggest a population wandering oblivious and anesthetized, removed from the sharper elements of the world—*La La Land, Lotus Land.* It stands against the notion that the metropolis is densely packed with *dreamers* who came to participate in *The Dream Factory* but will probably be disappointed (de-deluded), and

---

* Though this has long been the story, and I note that Wikipedia seems satisfied with it, some historians maintain that documents of the early 1780s signed by Spanish governor Felipe de Neve call the town simply *El Pueblo de la Reina de Los Angeles.* (Maybe they just shortened it for the documents?) In any case, it seems mystery, myth and expansive imaginings began to circle the settling early on.

wind up drifting down the *Boulevard of Broken Dreams*, whistling some West Coast version of "On Broadway."

I don't hear those terms floated as often as I did in the 80s. They may be fading, the popular utopian trope edged out by its evil twin, the even more popular dystopian L.A. The 2004 Oscar winner, *Crash*, set mostly in a gritty, nocturnal Los Angeles, used colliding cars as a metaphor for collisions between religious, racial and ethnic groups. (Interestingly, today Paul Haggis' story of conflict among various sects and factions—with instances of redemptive heroism and compassion—seems prophetic, but far more applicable to the global condition in general than to Los Angeles in particular.)

These darker, more considered perspectives have probably supplanted Woody Allen's 1970s-era vision of wide, sun-swept, palm tree-lined boulevards traveled by rather monochromatic-looking, wealthy people heading toward hillside homes where they'll chatter about film business over margaritas and scotch. Some of us will be grateful at least for that.

The poets of this collection are awake to their surroundings and—by evidence of numerous poems—alive to the "Beyond" that surrounds our surroundings. They are self-aware and world-aware. And they come from all over. The majority of poems here are not directly about the city or its outlying municipalities. The vast urbanscape roils with childhood and adolescent memories of other towns, states, others countries. There's Jawanza Dumisani's recollection of Detroit in the 60s, Mary-Alice Daniel's impressions of the South, Mary Armstrong's and B.H. Fairchild's true tales of the Midwest, Jackson Wheeler's riveting, breathless account of his family heritage and his upbringing in Southern Appalachia. (Toto,

xviii

we are *so* not on the MGM studio lot anymore). In critical studies, fiction and movies, the city is often analyzed or viewed as a thing apart, an anomaly, but the Los Angeles story is an American story.

And as for what we'd expect to see in a fat book of poems culled from L.A.? I have placed back-to-back a Carol Muske-Dukes poem that begins with two teenagers reclining poolside, studying a book on manners so as to compose a proper condolence note to an acquaintance who's suffered a death in the family, and Florence Weinberger's homage to people striving to maintain an ancient tradition that states the dead must be buried the day they died. They are gathering, piece by piece, "human remains" after the detonation of an explosive device. Smaller and smaller pieces.

Carol Muske-Dukes' poem may be the only one here that mentions a swimming pool. Oh those legendary swimming pools. (Funny, I don't see them around much anymore.) One poem in sunlight, the other in a landscape of horror, yet both are shadowed by an understanding of death, the dark knowing. The figures in some of the poems may be naïve, but the writers are not.

Although many of the emblems by which outsiders recognize L.A.—the Hollywood sign, the stars on the Boulevard, the Stahl House (Case Study House #22)—don't show up here, the characteristic images that do appear often take a different form, another shape, and are seen from an unexpected perspective. Only those who live here or have spent time in L.A. during the wet season know how palm fronds ripped off by winds lie all haywire across the streets in great, dripping, fleshy shapes— weirdly carnal. They don't look anything like what you'd expect. Hilda Weiss's poem notices that.

And then there are the freeways, which course through this collection as they do through the landscape. You don't need to have visited even once to know about the freeways. Except, I wonder, maybe those living elsewhere *don't* know. Do they understand about the *the?* San Franciscans, and apparently numerous folks from other cities, don't say *the.* They just say 'take 280 towards...' We'd never say 'take 405 to 10'—it's so impersonal. Here each freeway rises from the flat plane of the streets like the cut-out in a pop-up card, conveyed into three dimensions by that little *the.*

Do people elsewhere know that the 5, the 405, the 101, the twisty 110— first freeway in the American West (which in 1938 began as a "parkway" project then , mid-construction, was "quietly" reconceived as a freeway, until a recent historical preservation act changed the name to "Arroyo Seco *Parkway.*" But really it's still a freeway)*—do people elsewhere know these evoke for drivers a host of images and personal memories? Why, I could tell a story about the 10 that'd make even a non-driver sit bolt upright in amazement.

Meanwhile, "Car culture" can involve real culture inside the cars, be it high, low or mid. Music pours out of the dashboard, Hayden symphonies for Timothy Steele. And for Dana Gioia, a Beach Boys track rising from a shiny rental car returns him to a time when he'd drive his dad's beat-up Thunderbird to the beach.

* *Inventing Autotopia*, by Jeremiah B. C. Axelrod (U. of California), 2009, p. 302

One recurring element I did not predict, and I can only speculate on its meaning and implications. It's not present in a great many poems here, but enough so that the reader will find s/he keeps coming upon it in varying contextual arrangements, in poems of different language styles and moods. This element is religion, or rather *religions*—Christian, Jewish, Muslim, Islamic, and Hindu references, God and gods.

In the Los Angeles anthology I edited with Charles Webb in the 90s this was not so. A kind of spiritual longing, some sense of mystical engagement, did trace through *Grand Passion,* but it was rather non-specific.

It would seem something's changed between then and now. Maybe news of perilous battles overseas, conflicts involving ideology or religious rhetoric, and events that seems to draw nearer each day, are slipping across the collective conscience. Either that or these references have turned up by coincidence. (I'm a skeptic on many issues, but I do believe in coincidence.)

However it happened, in *Wide Awake* lines and references touching upon religion or the sacred—references serious or wistful, and some rather jolly— lie down together like lions and lambs engaged in some charming interspecies friendship. They have no quarrel with each other, but that's not to say the poems never come with an edge. The god prayed to in Yvonne Estrada's poem may not be a saving god—but with a kid's life on the line, a saving god is required.

Collectively, these poems endorse neither the dream nor the nightmare vision of Los Angeles. Instead they wander through absurdity, pathos, comedy, anguish, irony and tenderness. And through NELA, NoHo, West L.A., Venice West, Malibu, Hollywood, East Hollywood, Downtown, K-Town, J-Town, East Los and Leimert Park they wander, usually with a purpose.

Dave Jurasevich's photo shot from the Mt. Wilson Observatory cloaks all these neighborhoods, districts and particularities under a mantle of luminous, unearthly light. It's stunningly beautiful, but also alien, remote, untouchable. How can we know the people who live under that veil, which both illuminates and conceals? Small wonder movies cast the place as good or bad (or obviously bad v. secretly bad). What else could they do—straddle the two, or venture into some complicated middle ground and wind up not in a Crash but a Mishmash?

But the poems don't conform, don't line up squarely on this side or that. They labor on behalf of the angels, but might play a hand of gin rummy with the devil (well, *a* devil, one small, low-ranking devil). Or they're tricksters who carry a sorrow. They're both of Los Angeles yet outside it. The first one starts out on the freeway, eyes cast upward towards the rising hills, all aspiration and noble endeavor. The last winds up on foot, in flight, taking the poor kid's route through L.A. They're all over the place. They mess everything up. Naturally. They're *poems*. Thank goodness they don't have to pull in big bucks at the box office.

HILDA WEISS

Those Hills
Debs Park from the 110

One day, she says,
I will climb those hills
because they rise from the city
like shoulders.

See how they nudge the road?
They are zoo animals,
patient and harmless, behind the rope
of the highway.

But I have seen them
brass-back the sun like teenage boys
and cup the moon in their night dress
like your granny.

Pay attention as we come
around the curve. You will see
the muscle of a heart. That
is what hills are to the land.

They can teach you
to teach yourself.
That is why

you must climb with me
one day
those hills.

Hilda Weiss

Thumb in the Door

Sharp pain. A throbbing that lasted all night.
Blood under the nail. It quickly turned black.
You said: *How gross!*
Yes—

It's a working class thumb. A no-polish, cheap-girl thumb.
A thumb from a dirty house.
A farm girl thumb. A back country thumb.
A hick family thumb at the end of a long dirt road.

And, it's a Tomboy thumb.
A bleached hair thumb. A surfer girl thumb,
and, thank you, no makeup either thumb.

A long hike thumb. Yosemite climb thumb.
Wind in your hair thumb, and a sunburn scab
on your nose thumb. Even an old double-hung

window thumb. And yes, a daydreaming, oops, thumb.
A what-were-you-thinking? thumb. Oh,
Saturday afternoon. Almost summer.

In a musty garage. I don't remember
what I wanted, what I was reaching for.

Why the urgency to keep a door
from closing?

Hilda Weiss

Streetwise in LA

Of course they look like wings,
these long, dismembered arms blown down in the rain.
They crack like old shoe leather in the sun.

The sidewalk is crowded—
great shards, small chips, massive debris after
the wind of the night.

What do I see?
A mass of red fish, old roots,
a mermaid's hair spread out on the rocks.

Rudders and oars broken loose from a ship
and one lone wave rising off the meridian.
A pelvic bone. It could be a saddle.

The waist of one impaled on a fence.
A slide down cement steps.
Black pavement through a pianist's fingers.

Three forks, one spoon neatly stacked.
A battlefield of plows and rakes.
Too many palm fronds to trip on.

I cross the street.

MOLLY BENDALL

Pitch This

Where's my diagram to spiritual
        bliss?
                Under the roots?

Mandraked in a big cauldron?

           Coiffed in
seaweed? I'd make an easy do-it-yourself video
if only I had a camera.

    I'll sketch the calm. Beware of the dangers
of scurvy. I think sometimes the surfers

are out there, their black torsos against
           back-tongues of water, weighing the nothingness.
Talk about careers. There are new sounds

from the shallows, teasy pulls from the wind. I'll hold

    a microphone to record

        the splash, the streaks, the smithereens.

4

WILLIAM MOHR

In Line at Pancho's Tacos

At first I don't recognize him
walking through the door;
he owes me $75 from a year ago,
offers me his hand. I don't shake.
We talk. He's married and divorced,
going back to his first wife
whom he left nodding out at the piano.

"You still living at the same place?"
he asks, writing it down. "I'm expecting
a big check from back East, 2500,
by the end of the week."

"You got a phone?" I ask.
"No. I'm sort of moving around
right now." I grin, "Must be hard
for those social security checks
to keep up with you." He orders
a bean and cheese burrito,
then cancels it. I follow him outside.
New Jersey license plates.

One night he dropped a beer bottle
on the kitchen floor. Mid-morning
I walked in half-asleep, barefoot.
I missed a glass blade by a toe-length.

*

In fiction a writer's not supposed
to use real people. Your job's to create
new characters. In poetry, why lie —
if you're looking for a roommate,
don't let Nick DeNucci move in.

William Mohr

Big Band, Slow Dance

"Were you close?" I'm asked, as if grief
Would sting less deeply were we friends
As well as son and father. Further apart
Two men could never meet, though blood bends

Through arteries, veins and capillaries
Summoned into Presence by his pleasure.
Oh that I could have grown more slowly —
Remember being small and cradled like treasure.

One Miracle
for Bob Flanagan

Stunned by tequila from the night before,
I remember poking at embers as dawn
puffed its mist into a clearing. Bob sang
and coughed, sang and coughed. Even then,
I wondered how much longer he had.
Every time his body jerked, I winced.
I loved his improvised, contaminated genius.
Tonight he's in the hospital again, alone,
and this poem is like a waitress who deserves
a big tip—half the bill—for telling me
it's time to stop drinking coffee and drive over
and rescue him, perform the one miracle
I'm allowed in this life, but I'm not,
because Bob's not the one I'm supposed to save.

TONY BARNSTONE

The 167th Psalm of Elvis

Blessed are the marble breasts of Venus,
those ancient miracles, for they are upright and milk white
and they point above the heads of the crowd in the casino.
Blessed are the crowds that play, and whose reflections
sway in the polish of her eggshell eyes,
for they move in shimmers and flights of birds
as they circle the games, and they are beautiful and helpless.
Bless the fast glances that handle the waitress,
bless her miniskirt toga and the flame-gold scotch,
and bless the gamblers who gaze at the stage.
Remember also the dancer and remember her dance,
her long neck arched like a wild white goose,
the tassels on her nipples that shoot like sparks,
and bless the legs and bless the breasts
for they are fruit and honey and they are generous to the eyes.
Have mercy on my wallet, the dollars I punch into the slot,
and grace the wheels swapping clubs and hearts.
Mercy on me too, as I stumble as if in a hashish haze
watching the reels spin away, for I am a blown fuse
and I need someone to bless me before it's too late.
Honor the chance in a million, the slot machine jolting,
the yellow light flashing, honor the voice that calls *jackpot*,
and the coins that crush into the brushed steel tray,
for there is a time for winning and a time for losing
and if you cast your bread upon the waters
you will find it again after many days.
Pity the crowd around the blessed winner
all patting his back as if it rubs off,
this juice, this force, this whatever
that might save them from their own cursed luck.
And pity the poor winner whose hand claws back
into his bucket of coins and who cannot walk away,
because he'd do anything for the feeling
he had when the great pattern rose from the chaos
of cherries and lemons and diamonds and stars
and he knew for that moment he was blessed.

Tony Barnstone

The Californian Book of the Dead

I'm scared, so I'm writing this book of the dead,
a last testament, like James Kidd, Arizona prospector
mining the edge of Superstition Wilderness,
maybe murdered in Haunted Canyon for his gold,
whose will left his half million to research the spirit
because "I think in time we will photograph the soul
leaving the human at death." Perhaps we will, or perhaps
there's no will left when the body, sleeplike, settles
and the mind breaches, and the dendrites flaring in a final
visionary chain try to understand the storm wind ripping us
from our bodies, the million tiny Buddhas crawling down
the eyelids, white buddhas, red buddhas, blue and yellow.
The teenager daydreams super powers, walking invisible
into the girls' locker room and bank vaults, a super punch
that sends the football jocks sprawling, but doesn't dream
of the body's simplest power—the power to stop.
The body has its own will, and so I leave this testament.

Crack wide the doors of the sky, let my spirit leap
into heaven like a grasshopper, let me float among the stars
and eat the gods. When I stand before the lords of death
I'll testify that I leapt from the pit of dreams each morning
and tried to live my life awake, that I gave twenty dollars
to the woman by the freeway entrance with the *Homeless
and Humiliated* sign while the red truck honked behind me,
that I bowed my head and dug with my tongue
between my lover's legs, that I mined that cave
and the gold for me was the pleasure she felt, but I did not
sleep with that woman at the French bistro who was so bored
of her husband and her little girls. I lived the best I could.
And if the mind breaks down in death, and the last neuron
fires in darkness like a sun snuffed out in a dying galaxy,
and if I wander for a while alone and find no god,
no rat, no earthworm, no butterfly of the spirit realm,
then let this be my superpower, the ability to speak
without breath, to write without fingers, to streak like
a meteorite across a black screen, and to go on and on
without will or consciousness, just these dead words
dancing before your eyes, a toy skeleton on a string.

8

Tony Barnstone

Azusa Boulevard

I'm driving out the boulevard past icons,
orange planets floating over the gas
stations, the tiki-tiki lounge, the iron
sky, the convenience store where (for a pack
of cigarettes, eleven dollars and
a hat) the Pakistani clerk was shot
last week, the city like a void expanding
through the towns of lemonade, the lots
of polished marked-down cars below the freeway,
dark smog pushed against the hills, a fat
man to the table, galaxies of dust,
the low sky stained with nicotine and rust.
Los Angeles. A billboard explains that
Life Is Harsh. Your Tequila Shouldn't Be.

Tony Barnstone

Commandments

You shall visit a friend for dinner,
an amazing spread of food and drugs,
and you shall eat too much and you shall
smoke some dope, though it kills the memory,
and as your soul rises on a small metal rocket,
propelled by nitrous oxide into an airless seizure,
shuddering through something better than orgasm,
you shall imagine brain cells popping,
and you shall not care,
and when your friend's lover bends to pour
the wine, a little sloppy, flushed breasts
dropping from her open blouse, you shall not
look away, and when she catches your eyes
locked onto the brown gaze of her nipples
and smiles exhilarated with wine
and desire to see the bottle and glasses
and everything else in the fragile world
shatter and burn, you shall not be able
to keep from smiling back,
and you will drink too much, and you will fall
into the wineglass and into bed,
and you will taste grapes on her tongue,
salt on her thigh, breath in her breath,
and in the morning you will feel like hell
and you shall look in the mirror
at the vein flushing blue and rivering through
the puffed flesh beneath your eye,
and you will roll a dream of apples under your tongue
like a seed, how sweet the cut flesh,
the bulbs swelling red and yellow,
and you will worship her pomegranate lips,
her breasts like gazelles, her golden calves,
and you will tell yourself it is just two sacks
of bones and skin rubbing together like metal and flint,
and later you will call her, feeling helpless,
such is modern life, no white dove or rainbows,
no burning bush,
no mountaintop piercing the water,
just a voice from inside commanding you.

10

LINDA DOVE

St. Nicholas of Tolentino Spies a Palm Tree in the Storm Drain

The saint studies the man who cannot say no. He makes an effort to notice the man's desire, the way the man molds himself to whatever he craves so that the future settles in his pocket like loose change or lint or baby teeth. The man just wants what he wants, and so all objects could be one and the same. Doesn't everyone prefer to win? Even a palm tree will grow in a drain, feeding on run-off, a minor garden. The saint has his answer: it takes a year just to feel like he's not falling. How much longer until he can curve his body to the sun? Now is gone now. Now there are tumbleweeds in the city and birds roosting in the overpass. The weather forgets itself and wanders down the freeway unaware of what it used to know. Now there are a thousand words for snow.

Linda Dove

St. Nicholas of Tolentino Confronts His Moral Ambivalence in the Buffet Line

I grow weary seeing the vegetables,
boiled and cut, mashed, rubbed in oil

to within an inch of their pretty skins.
I have loved each one of them. Roots

hanging down into dirt as if the ground
held an eave of icicles. I tremble

at their dark reach. The carrot's orange
oblivion, the hoops of lavender around

the turnip head. Or the shiny froth of kale,
the way a cabbage cups its holy center.

I am not removed from their fanciful
life. I shuffle my tray along the line,

scooping warmed-over sides
onto my plate. I think of the garden,

the hot pink weight of a beet in hand.
I do not understand how this hunger

can be so easy. How I can suffer the leeks
to be sliced and scalded. How I do not

wither at the sight of the cucumber,
peeled back to its wet interior.

We settle our needs at our peril. I find
myself blaming the soul for language.

LIZ GONZALEZ

The Four Food Groups
in Grandma's Summer Lunches

L-
ard
fried thick
slabs of Spam,
toast brown, or eggs
scrambled with tuna or
canned green beans, or both.
Wash it down with powdered
milk stirred in tap water. Reboiled,
oversalted canned spinach. "You want
big muscles like Popeye's, don't you?"
And smashed wilted carrots for "20 / 20 dee-
veesion." Navel oranges, red apples, fingernail
beds of peels. Two slices of paper thin white bread.
"Eat all the food on your plate or you can't go outside
to play. The poor peckin' children are starving in China."

liz gonzalez

Espiritu

The voice in the receiver
a crackling memory
of the woman who once wore
hot pink velvet slippers
with a little heel
to clean the house
Telephones hold us close
She says I'm the only one
who calls to check-up on her
(But the others stop by)

Death sings from the rusting
rose garden in her front yard
The starched, dustless house
dissolves into gray peeling walls
Clumsy knees
won't let her cumbia
in the kitchen
No broken hips
God blesses her falls
The three-dimensional
bleeding Jesus
hangs above her bed
immaculate

Grandma's turned sweet
Soon, the white-winged owl
will light on her windowsill
Ninety-three is closer to finite
If I don't visit
I can look at her old pictures
remember her
the way she remembers herself
Belle of the barrio
The girl with Mary Pickford curls
dancing to the Beer Barrel Polka

At night, she sails a blessing
toward my city
From '63 to '71
she was my mother
Says she can't
keep alive for me forever
But we're not through yet
When she scolds me
I know she's staying
around a while

Fight with me Grandma
Call me *diablita*
Smack me with your fire

Confessions of a Pseudo-Chicana

Forgive me Our Lady of Guadalupe
for I have offended you.
It has been eight months
since I last lit a votive
or ate a bowl of menudo.
These are my sins:

I didn't taste chile until I was 18.
Mama raised us on Hamburger Helper
and macaroni & cheese.
She never even made a pot of beans.

I learned how to make tortillas
from Mrs. MacDougal in Home Ec.
Mama still has the recipe.

In high school, I bonged with Allman Brother
look-alikes and rocked out to Lynyrd Skynard
instead of suavecitoing to Malo & El Chicano.

After dancing at forty-nine weddings, I still
don't know what the lyrics to "Sabon A Mi" mean.
(I can't even speak fluent Spanglish.)

liz gonzalez

Most of my friends who carry green cards
flew in from the blue-eyed countries.

The closest I got to a protest march
was rushing the gates at the Lilith fair.

My biggest sin—I buy grapes. But only
organically grown from Wild Oats.

Forgive me Madre Maria.
I was brought up by a mama who thought Chicana
was a dirty word, and a grandma
who claims she's *I*-talian.

Help me from turning into
a vendida with blue contacts,
and never let me forget that

great grandpas' sweat glistens
on the metal of Santa Fe railroad tracks;

good old boys brand and corral primos
like cattle they own and slaughter;

ninas stitch arthritis into their fingers
inside malquiladoras;

tios' skin, eyes, lungs
get fumigated with pesticides every day.

Madre Maria, instead of kindling
candles with your image to look cool,
I'll light the wicks in remembrance of them.

SHOLEH WOLPÈ

The Outsider

I know what it's like to be an outsider.

I know how English sounds
when every word is only music.

I know how it feels not
to be an American, an English, a French.
Call them
       Kharejee— Amrikayee, Ingleesee, Faransavi,
see them
       see me as alien, immigrant, *Iranee.*

But I've been here too long.
I am now an American
      with an American husband
      and American children…

But mark this—I do not belong anywhere.
I have an accent in every language I speak.

Sholeh Wolpé

How Hard Is It to Write a Love Song?

Last night a sparrow flew into my house,
crashed against the skylight and died:
I want to write a love song.

Poppy seed cake on china plate,
tea like auburn gold, the *New York Times*
open on the table, black with news,
and the man I still love with me.

The newspaper says in Conakry a man is
sticking his Kalashnikov into a woman. Now
he's pulling the trigger.

Hummingbirds zip through the garden.
My lover slowly rocks in the hammock,
a spy novel on his stomach.

I flip a page and a Nigerian soldier
shoots a man because he's parked badly,
and takes the dead man's hat.

The bougainvillea has burst into pinks and reds,
the colors of Kabul's sidewalks after a suicide attack.
The child next door squeals with laughter.

How hard is it to write a love song?
A little in-the-moment swim,
a bit of Bach—perhaps.

GERALD LOCKLIN

Green Corn Tamales

First in Tucson,
Now at El Cholo in L.A.,
On Western just south of Olympic,
My wife and I make a point
Of enjoying them once a summer.

All tamales are not hot.
These are sweet with the syrup
Of young corn, steamed within
The husks. Even the thin strand
Of a green pepper seems sweet.
Even the morsel of tender chicken
Seems sweet.

Sweet as sweethearts
On the evening promenade
Above the beach at Mazatlan.
Sweet as summer evenings.
Sweet as the respite, the
Renewal, at the end of day.

Think sweetly of green corn tamales,
Remembering that the water of the desert,
Hoarded by the thirsty cactus,
Is the sweetest water.

Gerald Locklin

I've Always Enjoyed Her Sense of Humor

She's an old friend
And I don't see her very often,
But she has a way of showing up
When I'm talking to a girl I've just met,

And she will invariably storm up to us
And confront me with,
"Where is the child support check?!"

Then turn on her heel and storm from the room,
Leaving me to make inadequate explanations.

AMY UYEMATSU

The Accusation

my husband tells me I'm crazy but I've got eyes
he's just like my Jose back home
only thinks of one thing
little girls old ladies same
once we driving on the highway I catch
him leering at woman must be 80 or more
'stop the car' I command
nearly fall out the door, leave him for good
but he says I'm the only one
and I want to believe
after all we've only been married two years
he tells me he'd given up looking
him already 76 when we met
and me 51 when I became wife number four
love real happy for a while
he takes me to Las Vegas and I get to play
everyday the quarter video game
I always select the same machine
I swear it likes me best
since I always win 5, 10, even 20 dollars
while people around me sour
about these one-armed bandits
but my husband says our hotel bill
is getting 'out-of-hand' so we come back
and I'm all the time bored
I cook and clean and water my potted plants
still too much time so I do the morning crossword
proud my English is good enough to fill the blanks
I gossip with Manila girlfriends
e-mail sisters in Hawaii and France

I crochet dresses for my growing rack of blue-
eyed dolls from 99-cent store
no matter how busy I can't forget
that picture of his wife
in the box on top cupboard shelf
the first time I see her I cry
'look at her' is all I can say

Amy Uyematsu

I almost tear the photo to shreds
but my husband calls me silly
'she's old now all white-haired
who doesn't turn any more heads'
lucky for me I still do with tight
black slacks and sling-back pumps
my husband says it makes him proud
to have me at his side
but I know how all of them think
and my husband no better
all the time I watch him close
like last week he sneaks our shopping cart
to a different line
claims a shorter wait
who does he think he's fooling
I can see his eyes undressing
the smiling checker
I yell at him all the way home
he insists 'I'm innocent'
even laughs at my upset
so mean to flaunt
that filthy heart
why should I trust when
just this morning he clicks on t.v.
to women's soccer finals
I rush over to block the screen
'you're disgusting' I scream
lusting at those teen-age girls'
I make him turn it off
my outrage quickly turns to pleas
all I'm asking for is one
just one good man
who'll just be only mine

Kickball

I think I'm finally getting it, not just getting by but really getting it – you dig –so I can put down my guard, maybe dance a little reckless, cruise toward home plate knowing no danger's in sight. In sight. Now that's where the trouble begins. I should rely more on insight— full-of-grizzle-and-blood-strength insight. You'd think I'd been tripped enough times by now to know when the enemy's just waiting, but naiveté can blind one girl's eyes as much as mistrust does the next girl's. Three time's the charm is always way too few in my book. My life should be called "Gullible's Travels." Even my own kid gets mad at me when I don't turn my emotional dial up to scorn and revenge or at least self-preservation. But no, I don't see the knife coming. Those poison letters would be neon signs for most. Instead I hear one more lie then nearly slice off my finger while carving the Thanksgiving turkey. I may as well be back in the first grade, swinging contentedly while floating up toward the sky as the kickball comes out of nowhere, strikes between my two eyes—a perfect hit.

AMÉLIE FRANK

It Came to Pass in a Backyard in Silverlake

Not an Atlas Shrugged joke.
Not the North Pole at two o'clock.
Not a gazing ball misadventure.
Not the best way to prognosticate
where the next, best strike will come.
Not an error made
while God played jacks with the universe.
Not ribbed for your pleasure, her surfaces.
Not widowed of axis, her kilter.
Not pregnant with fiery juice, her core.
Not craving her miscarried offspring, her moon.
Not playing coy with her icy bottom.
Not tossed away for a better Jupiter, or a shot
at spontaneously generated Venus.
Not a cheap quip about the abstract meeting
the concrete.

It took days and days for her to get across
this stretch of the backyard. Time for the weeds
to stretch up, embrace, and circumnavigate.

TERRY WOLVERTON

Paradox

In the midst of singing is silence,
small gaps of breath. The billowed lung soon
empties of its air. Every thing
contains its opposite: Love changes
its blouse to emerge as loathing; good
fortune shrivels to despair. That star
we yearn toward is the radiance
we fear. Haunted by what we've escaped,
we cling to overstuffed suitcases
that open to reveal the void
we carry everywhere. Shadow
can't survive without the sun's bright beam,
and death holds life in its coat pocket,
fingers stroke it like a lucky charm.

Hopscotch Highway

I should have known better than to wear
the ball gown, the one with a tight waist.
I sweat orange circles into that red
taffeta; my chignon combusted
in the blue wind. I stuck out my thumb
and the sky sneered. Overhead, the crows
were sympathetic, but we all knew
no one luminous was going to pass
this way, not before the gold storm rose.

That moon, she couldn't do a damn thing
for me. I had a rocket in my
belly; I wanted to savor her
from afar. How will I know my heart's
broken? If we come here with just so
many breaths, maybe we come with just
so many tears. Maybe I've dried up,
a lake that's disappeared, residue
of fish bones glinting under the sand.

In Praise of Jokes

Two musicians are driving when they notice the Grim Reaper in the back seat. Why do bald people put holes in their pockets? The CIA had an opening for an assassin. Why don't cannibals eat clowns? A guy comes walking into a bar with a turtle on his head. A man has a dog that snores in his sleep. A farmer has 200 hens and no rooster. A frog telephones the Psychic Hotline. How do you make a blonde laugh on Saturday? Descartes is sitting in a bar, having a drink. Adam was walking around the garden of Eden, moping. A boy prayed for two weeks for $100 but nothing happened. What does an atheist say when she's having an orgasm? A woman is learning to golf. A petty thief, a teacher, and lawyer die and go to heaven. A distraught man goes to see a psychologist. Adolf Hitler went to see a fortune-teller. How many surrealists does it take to change a light bulb? Doctor, doctor, I have 59 seconds to live.

Terry Wolverton

In Praise of Traffic on the 405

Wheels tell wind who gone. It's always rush hour on the 405. One hour seeps into next, steady exodus from north to south and back again. We yearn to go, but freeway holds us earthbound, suspended. Rush hour is not happy hour. Ten wide lanes of momentum thwarted, unasked for stay. Deprived of destination. Captive witness to vistas beyond the glass: hoods of broken-downs gaping like beaks of giant metal birds, brutal ballets of collision, fire scorching up the stretch of hillside, woman in the front seat screaming. But it's not rush hour that makes us scream. Traffic lubricates, allows this sound to erupt from the dark prison where we keep it locked, buoys it past the iron gate of our lips. Without this unscheduled pause for screaming, we would implode. Roll down your window and sing.

WANDA COLEMAN

I Live for My Car

can't let go of it. to live is to drive. to have it function
smooth, flawless. to rise with morning and have it start
i pray to the mechanic for heat again and air conditioning
when i meet people i used to know i'm glad to see them until
i remember what i'm driving and am afraid they'll go outside and
see me climb into that struggle buggy and laugh deep long loud

i've become very proficient at keeping my car running. i
visit service stations and repair shops often which is why
i haven't a coat to wear or nice clothes or enough money each
month to pay the rent. I don't like my car to be dirty. i spend
saturday mornings scrubbing it down. i've promised it a new bumper
and a paint job. luckily this year i was able to pay registration

i dream that my car is transformed into a stylish
convertible and i'm riding along happily beneath sun glasses
the desert wind kissing my face my man beside me. we smile
we are very beautiful. sometimes the dreams become nightmares
i'm careening into an intersection the kids in the back seat scream
"mama!" i mash down on the brake. the pedal goes to the floor

i have frequent fantasies about running over people i don't like
with my car

my car's an absolute necessity in this city of cars where
you come to know people best by how they maneuver on the freeway
make lane changes or handle off-ramps. i've promised myself
i will one day own a luxury model. it'll be something
i can leave my children. till then i'm on spark plugs and lug nuts
keeping the one i have mobile. i live for it. can't let go of it
to drive is to live

Wanda Coleman

Wanda Why Aren't You Dead

wanda when are you gonna wear your hair down
wanda. that's a whore's name
wanda why ain't you rich
wanda you know no man in his right mind want a
          ready-made family
why don't you lose weight
wanda why are you so angry
how come your feet are so goddamn big
can't you afford to move out of this hell hole
if i were you were you were you
wanda what is it like being black
i hear you don't like black men
tell me you're ac/dc. tell me you're a nympho. tell me you're
          into chains
wanda i don't think you really mean that
you're joking. girl, you crazy
wanda *what* makes you so angry
wanda i think you need this
wanda you have no humor in you you too serious
wanda i didn't know i was hurting you
that was an accident
wanda i know what you're thinking
wanda i don't think they'll take that off of you

wanda why are you so angry

i'm sorry i didn't remember that that that
that that that was so important to you

wanda you're ALWAYS on the attack

wanda wanda wanda i wonder

why ain't you dead

29

Wanda Coleman

Sonnet for Austin
—After a line by E. Ethelbert Miller

I love you as the grave loves the stone

I do not love you as if you were salt-pork or opal
or the sorrow of grass widows tending fields.
I love you as uncertain fingers foil tenderness
in public, where all eyes witness our covetings.

I love you as the wind loves the tumbleweed
and carries it across the sand to its lair of secrets.
I love you as chocolate loves cinnamon risen
from my breath to revive the poem in your eyes.

I love you as today loves yesterday—the way Billie loved Prez

Wanda Coleman

Neruda

few quiet hours
i spend them soaking in the tub with my neruda

in a dream a bearded moreno stranger
approaches me along a dark street in the plaza
as we pass he whispers hoarsely, "neruda"

on sunset boulevard a beggar accosts me
for spare change.   i hand him my collected neruda

while my lover takes siesta i walk down to
the neighborhood bar for a game of pool solo. i order
dos besos. i put a quarter in the juke and notice
all selections read neruda

while standing at the supermarket checkout stand
i read tabloid headlines. one screams
"man force-feeds wife neruda"

(he tells me he is worried neruda is coming between us)

note found in cantonese fortune cookie:
neruda slept here

FLORENCE WEINBERGER

Lunatics Love Neruda

Twenty years apart, two lunatics gave me copies of Pablo Neruda's *Twenty Love Poems and a Song of Despair*. Inscribed them with tidings straight out of their soiled hearts. One swore not to hurt me, and branded me with scars of betrayal, which I sometimes pass along. The other scribbled Greek or Hebrew letters across the first four pages, who could tell what from what, their scattered angles obscuring their truth. He'd walked out of Barnes and Noble without paying for the book, a small crime in context. Should I not be grateful each year swallows the years that have gone before? Time passes otherwise undigested, in break-out flash-backs. One day, filing like a librarian instead of a fatalist, I come across the two books, as if one had given birth to the other, their twinned presence reminding me I'd never read Neruda's love poems! What a morning, to be granted a second chance, to read the master in maturity. To be given the gift of pause. To pardon the reckless promises humans make in unguarded handwriting. Age makes desire manageable. It is possible to visit Neruda for the first time, possible to fall into his mercy, the way I dropped from the womb into somebody's outstretched arms.

Florence Weinberger

The Light Gatherers

In their passion for completion, the devoted—dry-lidded,
holy and haunted—poke among the blasted pieces
for traces of what newspapers call "human remains"
but something, of course, will always be missing.

Impossible to get it all. All that once had a semblance
reassembled to be buried close to wholeness. As if they
can ever resemble themselves again. Leg by cell by eyelash,
they will be gleaned by the *hesed shel emet*

faithful who are hoisted aloft to lift human flesh
off the trembling leaves. Before the last light, the first star,
they will sift the shards of colossal explosives,
combing through tangles of rubber, singed wire,

glass, shoes, the body shells, every crumb of skin,
ash of hair, finger nail, the clotted blood, the cracked skull,
the broken armature of bones; they will climb the sides
of buildings carrying plastic bags filled with cotton balls

to blot the stunned bricks, the smoking windows.
While dazed mourners try to find a *minyan*, they will pick
at the bark of trees, scour flag poles, every house and lamp post
they pass to bundle up what once were children—

there are always children—busy women who shopped early
for produce still livid with soil, readers and smokers and men
who sold diamonds. Even if these burial crews come home
to their wives washed clean,

who wants a job like this, without pay, restless, sleepless,
their fingernails cut to the quick, their pockets emptied.
It is not written *You shall bury him intact,*
only *You shall bury him on the day he dies.* To do it right,

they would have to save the very air around the deed,
even the man who strapped explosives to his chest.
His severed head. His squandered heart.
Everything that belongs to each dead. The last blood

that leaves the body contains the soul, it is written.
The last breath contains the awe, the last sight an after-
image that cannot be imagined. Once bound to the task,
they must gather with charity all that is commingled: the killer

and the killed, when one left home to board the bus,
the bomb hidden, the infant held, the terrible misconception
of the teaching, the non-believer settled in beside the devout,
the words they were about to utter to each other,

the sweet subtext of country. This is not a country easily divided
from the body. Because every Jew carries it, it scatters;
Jews have been found in cellars, their scrolls in caves,
their rituals in Mexico. An exploded bus is a Torah destroyed.

The gatherers, meticulous to the point of madness, are like
crows in the field. Avid and silent at their work, they bring back
to their young their stories which are passed *l'dor va dor*
from mouth to mouth to mouth...........

CAROL MUSKE-DUKES

Condolence Note: Los Angeles

The sky is desert blue,
Like the pool. Secluded.
No swimmers here. No smog –

Unless you count this twisting
Brushfire in the hills. Two kids
Sit, head to head, pool-side,

Rehearsing a condolence note.
Someone has died, "Not an intimate,
Perhaps a family friend", prompts

The Manners Guide they consult.
You shouldn't say *God never makes
Mistakes,* she quotes, snapping her

Bikini top. Right, he adds – You
Could just say, *He's better off* –or
Heaven was always in his future.

There's always a better way to say
"We're sorry that he's dead" – but
they're back inside their music now,

Pages of politeness fallen between them.
O do not say that the Unsaid drifts over us
Like blown smoke: a single spark erupts

In wildfire! Cup your hands, blow out
This wish for insight. Say: Forgive me
For living when you are dead. Say pardon

My need to praise, without you, this bright
Morning sky. It belongs to no one—
But I offer it to you, heaven in your future—

Along with silent tunes from the playlist,
the end-time etiquette book dropped
From the hand of the young sleeper.

It's all we have left to share. the book
Of paid respects, the morning's hot-blue
I-pod, sunlit words on a page, black border.

After Skate

He glides in on his single wing, after the signs go up. After
the truck leaves with the bunkbeds, grill, broken hall mirror.
After Scout is dropped off at the shelter. After the last look,

on the dying lawn. In the backyard, where the empty pool
stands open; he pops an ollie over the cracked patterns of tile:
tidal waves in neat squares. He kneels, checking angle against

depth. He lifts off where the board once leapt and leapt: cannon-
balls, swans: endless summer. He hurtles downward, kickturning,
sparks grinding hard on gunnite. Round the bend: the kidney,

the heart. The stone path where once glowed tiki torches at
the kingdom's ukelele gate. He rockets out of the dead lots each
day, past swingsets and shut-off sprinklers, his board struck up

from whirlwind. Nobody's home to the ownerless: he turns
inside their names, never minds ghosts, nothing in his wake.

Carol Muske-Dukes

Twin Tree

A tree divided. It grew like that—
Its slender trunk suddenly forking,

Lifting up from the crux in two Shiva arms—
As if it had come to a crossroads and split

The way twins unpeel from one another
In the womb. Two from one, it reached up

And flourished this way— it topped thirty feet
As its thick dark glossy leaves, half-folded like

Paper boats, kept the nubs of coming pears
Hidden then dangling. Avocado, avocado.

I held you in my hand as a big wrinkled pit,
Propped you, (as I'd been taught once by a lover

Who was trouble) with four toothpicks over a glass
Filled with water—till the tiny white filament inside

Your worried seed slowly let itself down into the
Clear transparency, while sprouting above into a

Green feasible stem. I transplanted those floating roots,
The top-heavy shoot after weeks—then waited till it

Reached out at last– growing fast in both directions,
Down into dirt, up into the sky over the backyard. When

It twinned, climbing upward, I stopped my husband,
Standing hard by with a shears, from pruning it back

Into one: *The only way it would survive* he said. But
It doubled skyward into the single tree at the top—

A hermaphrodite—as it had to be to make fruit. So
Many alligator pears, summer after L.A. summer! We

Carol Muske-Dukes

Filled baskets with the abundance of the you
And you: the fruit of two separate flowerings

From one quick hesitation. Till days after David died,
When clumsy workmen, digging a trench, severed your

Taproot. I saw the white exposed arteries they'd chopped clean
With their spades. I stood beside you weeping, trying to hold

Your heart together with my hands at the fork where you'd
Leaned apart, then towered. You were my love, conflict tree, –

Tough-skinned, the rich light-green flesh beneath. Avocado,
They killed you. When we sold the house, you were a cut stump.

DAVID HERNANDEZ

Huntington Botanical Gardens

Boring for a boy: 150 acres
and one hundred times as many plants,
each flouncing its colors. He drags
his bones where his parents want to go.
Here's the Japanese Garden,
a red bridge arcing from green lawn

to green lawn, blood orange carp
fishtailing sluggishly in the pond.
Here's the Subtropical Garden's
fat leaves, blue jacarandas and pink
cape chestnuts. Here's a yawn
blooming on the boy's face,
black petals rimmed with white teeth.

Mother whiffs a rose. Father snaps
a photograph of a peacock
unfurling its emerald feathers.
Too dull for a boy, watching nature
on display like this, flamboyant
and rainbowed like this.

It's all humdrum until the cacti
at the Desert Garden, their million
pinpricks. Walking the narrow
stone path, the boy never felt his skin
this way, so much hazard so close,
the thin hairs on his forearms rising.

A girl scurries by. Her mother
shouts from behind, *Don't run!*

He will remember this. After each
failed relationship and gray silence
that followed, this: the girl's palm
and fingers bristling with needles,
a cactus missing a handful of spines.

David Hernandez

Dear Professor

Let me explain my lengthy absence—
My entire family got food poisoning,
myself included. We had eaten rotten
fish tacos, old bad cod, I've never been so
nauseous, the house wouldn't stop
spinning, wouldn't stop shuffling
its windows, I was gushing from
I'll spare you the details. And Grandma
shutting down, hallucinating, said the world
was pixilated. We rushed her to St. Mary's
on a flat tire, no spare in the trunk,
a burst of sparks as the screaming rim
scored the road like a pizza cutter.
They plugged her in, her monitor drew
neon green mountain ranges. Strange,
you'd think they'd have Internet access
there, free wi-fi, a wing in the hospital
to check one's email. Odd, too, no
connectivity back home, no electric blood
sluicing through the wires, a hitch
in the system, some inexplicable glitch,
impossible for me to get a hold of you
until now, two weeks after the due date.
I'm sorry. And sorry I missed class today,
another flat tire, stupid overturned
box of nails on the freeway, I hissed
for miles, the car listed, such a headache,
and still queasy from the tacos. Please
consider all this when grading my essay
(see attachment). Please excuse any typos
or logical fallacies, my mind has been
elsewhere: Grandma's mountains
stretched flat. Her green horizon. I want
to live forever. I want to pass your class
and graduate, get a gig, marry some hottie,
see the world, drive until my wheels
come wobbling off, and keep driving—
but first I need to pass your class.
No pressure. Honestly. No pressure.

40

David Hernandez

Against Erosion

Certain is the surgeon in his surgical gown
as the scalpel enters the swabbed flesh
of the woman in the surgical light.
How intimate is all the pulling, fingers
massaging her face, the slackening
skin tucked like a bed sheet.
Two days before stitches are clipped,
railroading around her crown.
Gone a decade into the curls of hair,
the dread of cameras and mirrors.

A woman makes certain strides
past the sliding gaze of certain men,
their whistles and sighs and double-
takes, but soon winter goes, spring
resurrects green. Swiftly the seasons
undress, months peel from the wall,
and newer wrinkles crease the flesh.
Gone the comfortable lead ahead of time,
the sprightly bounce in her footsteps

before a pen glides along her face again.
Anesthesia brings a dream of waves
destroying a shore. A safeguard tower
kneels to the water, beach umbrellas
swept and pinwheeling. Gone the slabs
of cliff, the cypress trees, guardrail
and road. Gone the surrendering earth
into the colossal blue where it was born.

David Hernandez

Planting the Palms

Wednesday, they begin digging the holes.
Thursday, they kept digging, each man's legs

lost in the ditch of their making, orange vests
vanishing underground after every shovelful.

Nineteen palm trees lie across the vacant lot
until the crane arrives, until one by one

they're lifted. It's sexual how they rise
before the men, their roots caked in dirt.

But now it's Saturday. I've just folded up
the paper, the rape still chilling my skin.

One girl, five men, their zippers unclenching
their teeth. From the window I can see

all nineteen palms stationed along the blacktop,
fronds tied up in green ponytails. I'm amazed

at our hands, what ten could do to a girl.
Only a breeze drifting in from the Pacific,

but still I'm reminded of a hurricane,
of a world dropped into a blender: black wind,

rain falling sideways, a roof unhinged
and flipping end over end like a playing card.

Everything breaking apart except the palms,
an entire row gently bending into prayer.

MARSHA DE LA O

Janet Leigh Is Afraid of Jazz
—For Eddie Muller

The voices that swim through the music
offering something forbidden, close-up,
the dark arms of the horn player, his skin
fitting him sleek as a shark suit, clasping
the sax lifting it as sound descends
in long sizzling lines like wires arcing out,
empty eye sliding up and back
to the halo of the spot, motes drifting.
It makes her want to run. Like it could tear her
apart, a man at each limb lifting her
off the bed at the Otay Mesa motel,
all of them dressed in black and the music
never letting up its dazzling spun-out
phrases. If she could run, she would, under
the shadowy arcade as the camera pans wide
but she's hobbled by her tight skirt,
the staccato of high heels tapping
a rhythm on the uneven street,
her breasts heaving under cashmere,
dog collar of pearls around her perfect
neck while the sea crashes in the near
distance. We know she's doomed by music,
cloudburst of percussion on the windshield
then silence, the camera wheels around
and Bates Motel appears, lit up on the sign.
It's the way every aperture turns
into another eye and the shower
won't stop running until long after
she's died. We know she's doomed, chords
shifting darkly, but she persists,
carrying on with her share of sorrow,
changing into black lingerie and
skipping town if she has to, ending
finally there, wherever the
heart of trouble happens to be.

Marsha de la O

Chinese Lantern

There was only one place we ever ate Chinese,
Lin's on Los Feliz,

my grandfather ruling the table
with the same almond chicken, egg foo young,

little saucers of hot mustard. In the ceiling
they'd mounted a Chinese lantern with red tassels,

a kind of three-story castle clinging upside down
to the roof of heaven.

Depending where we sat, my sisters and I could watch lit scenes
in each castle wall—a maiden crossing a footbridge

peach trees in blossom, two birds
on a branch leaning toward each other,

a river tumbling like raw silk through a gorge.
I always wanted to watch the birds, wanted

only the maroon booth in the back, not the ebony chairs
and so did my cousin Deidre who wore plum-colored

lipstick and teased her hair—*they're love doves,*
she whispered from the high throne of high school,

ginger and garlic rousing my mouth. The next time
we saw her there, months later, Deidre was sway-backed

and swag-bellied, her eyes sad and defiant at once,
hand pressed to the small of her back, a silver moon

pendant shining between mountains of bosom.
She watched the lovebirds and didn't say anything.

I can see it now, my mother's face
twisting a wind that scatters all words,

44

Marsha de la O

Deidre's wet eyes and the birds leaning in,
quiet after the tumult of love.

That night I felt a bird enter and sink down
through me, the bird that is thirst,

the bird that can drink an ocean and not be quenched,
because thirst is both wanting and water

and water doesn't want to stop,
water wants to let it happen

the way Deidre let it happen, deliberately,
one step after another crossing a bridge,

her eyes glassy with knowledge and so quiet afterwards,
I saw what she'd been looking at all that time,

the wings of two birds going so fast—
a blur of stillness,

water roaring through a gorge
each droplet's great quiet flight

silence,
like when your mother calls out,

her voice dark with suspicion,
what are you doing in there

and you answer *nothing*

Blue Parrots

Some lunge at each other's throat, others blare
their klaxon horns, quarreling for the roost
because desire is a terrible thing, each crook
more brilliant than the next. The nets mesh the air
spread over the blue like a snare in heaven.
Years ago in another aviary, I'd sit like this
without moving for hours, I'd trained myself.
Here, flamingos dizzy with lice, their beaks'
chisels open and close on what's not there
but that's all part of it, this squawk and sputter
after pure space in the canopy, the way parrots
want flight and wanting should be spare and
made of nothing but a woven wire, a door,
an outer door, two locks. I've gone through
that threshold into shadow, but what violet
what blue compromise with the steel and cobalt
of night—for this it is said, *entertain strangers*
for this the match flares in bars of yellow and
blue, for many have entertained angels unawares,
flameburst of radium and bone, helpless, undone,
you drop everything, it all falls away, and when
you come to, you're holding hands with the
wrong stranger, it's like that

To Go to Riverside

Picture a boy,
    a smooth stone cupped in his hand—
  he's the boy David, or maybe it's a gun

    flat against his palm, and he's an archangel
    aiming for the darkened windows
  of the church. First the blast, then the shattering,

    the slap of running feet,

he never turned to see the windows fall,
    falling inside solder lines, inside lead lines
  unless the caliber was small and only

    left a bunghole of white light.
    It could have happened that way. That's why
  my father went to Riverside to make repairs

    because a saint shattered

a woman kneeling with oils or a man reaching
    for the wounds, the five glorious fountains.
  Our father took the whole family to the Inland Empire

    where groves were laid down in all directions
    like the careful quilting of God.
  Robber barons built their mansions

    and the fields of the Lord were planted in citrus.

Churches reared straight up and were shot
    through by boys. We spent our first vacation
  at the Sleepy Bear while our father ministered

    to a fallen window and we threw ourselves over
    and over in the bleached water of the pool,
  hot dirty light shafting down on our heads.

Marsha de la O

Years later I went back to Riverside

and met a man who brought me to his house.
　　He'd been shot in the chest, a large caliber
weapon, and when he took his shirt off,

　　his skin was still surprised, an epicenter
　　and ripples, all of it scar. I wanted
to see the exit wound, but couldn't ask.

　　I wanted to see the actual damage,

the way the body took it, the light in the church
　　when no one is there but the glazier
and his small daughter, a girl not left behind

　　to throw herself against the flat slap
　　of water, eyes rimmed red
with bleach, a plume from the steel mill

　　above our heads, one great chimney

called Bess towering over the blast furnace
　　and many coking ovens
without names, the leaves of the orange

　　trees in Fontana already blackened.
　　They harvested the last grapefruit
during the second World War, after that

　　the trees couldn't give anymore.

To go to Riverside when churches
　　were stoned and men
were shattered. I imagine my father

　　on scaffolding, his careful hands,
　　the way the three women were tender
taking down the crucified Christ

　　and their tenderness made the soldiers afraid.

48

KATE GALE

Corn

The floor was full of corn and my breath of silences.
The leaves were gold, red, orange. I wanted blue,
but there were none. My legs were blue where you slapped me,
but we leaned into corn night after night. The arc
of the moon appearing finally, the husks gathered into fire.

The corn husking lasted weeks. My shoulders bare
and whipped along the blades. August burned and blistered.
Corn and sorrow taste salty along the rim of the tongue.
You, coming apart at the seams. The kernels so packed on the ears,
milky sweet, that when you bit them, they fairly burst.

Roasted with salt they were a direction for life, salt water and fire.
I couldn't imagine growing away then. Outside the circle of firelight
was unimaginable blackness. Inside, the rain of blows, your hands hard
and heavy, corn that would give way to fall
apple picking in the orchard by the stream.

Much later I understood that people dream of life by a stream in a corn
field. What they wished for I could not imagine.
The vultures were always there overhead when we husked.
I imagined you would kill me some day.
Afterlife would be an adventure for me, and a meal for the vultures, surely.

Kate Gale

Everyone Has a House

What I like about your country
she tells me is the toilets
I wouldn't mind bringing one home
but it wouldn't do much good
she says she likes the bathtubs
and the refrigerators
but she is not so crazy
about the tortillas
which are not made properly
or the cilantro which tastes like soap
Also the freeways ruin the landscape
and the children watch television
when they could be playing soccer
and the teenagers stare at their parents
with bare faces that say
give it to me
and the abuelitos are like dogs
to the children
the children walk by with no respect
mangoes here are not so good
not enough rain
and the women here have so many clothes
I think your country has the most wonderful bathrooms
and everyone has a house
although tents would be nicer
I think or boats
or even just sleeping in a tree
My family has a tree
we live under
but the tree has no toilet
I grant you that.

CONNEY WILLIAMS

recuerdo

i wonder if Fidel
hears the wheezing of Che'
when he sleeps in his jungle house
with neither cocoa leaves or vines
when the green of Cuba
creeps into his breathing
choking his compatriot
even in death
will he make him give another speech
to unite nations of islands
rally his rebel Corazon
until Bautista agrees to return
and fight him face to face
like despots never do
maybe Che' wouldn't have gone to Angola
or Bolivia
maybe Che' would have lived
long enough to die of natural causes
like Fidel did in 1960
esperanza was tucked within the bough
as they walked the slippery decks
beneath that swollen Caribbean moon
that slow boat ride
from Mexico to Cienfuegos to Santiago
clouds of cohiba waft like halos
from their hard tobacco conversation
the salty wet crash upon the playas
scream like brown pelican for libertad
sometimes friends forget
sometimes they forget why they were friends
what made the affection so tender
and the air melt like a spider web
in the rain between them
it wasn't that they both rode
reddish brown stallions
through trails only they knew
or holstered the same german pistols
maybe it was the softness of Fidel's kiss

Conney Williams

whenever the reaper would try to strangle
daylight from the diamonds in Che's eyes
their sparkle receding into dark mines
that had never know liberation
it's possible Fidel wishes to see
the unevenness of Che's facial hair
all of his bones intact
the way they were before they returned
to his adopted home 30 years later
so dry and brittle
with no fight left in them
if it is true that hubris and strokes
have not stolen the clarity of Fidel's first vision
and lush love
that he shared with that Argentine physician
who surrendered his love for motor bikes
for a new country and Bolivian sleep
maybe Fidel does remember a beret's honesty
and just how tight its manifesto fits

WENDY C. ORTIZ

Some Scars

He went away to El Salvador the last summer of us,
and I stayed behind. While he assisted in elections with the threat

of bombs, I was spinning loose, taking jogs around the lake
after which I'd have a beer and cigarette. Pieces

of myself were lost around that lake. I pulled all-nighters
and brought a friend home with me after hours of dancing.

It was important that I remove the smoke from the bar
so I took a shower by candlelight, my friend

watching, blowing out the flame. The smoke washed down the drain.
Satisfied, I led my friend to bed, and the room glowed with the undoing.

The instant I met his eyes at the airport, he knew. Like good
radicals, we fought until we came to some arrangement we thought

we could live with. Our life together became one of airport runs
and steamed-up car windows, shouting in bedrooms, sobbing, folded up

on nicked hardwood floors. I came home to a bedroom of confetti:
my love notes turned on me. Loose on my hips, his green jeans

came off for others, often.
Then someone new caught my eye

and I raced toward that new fire with the thorny burrs of old, gnarled
    love
still stuck to me. Look here: I have the scars to prove it.

Wendy C. Ortiz

Accused 1 & 2

In 2003, three people, two of whom were California Institute of Technology graduate students, protested the American auto industry's contribution to environmental pollution by using Molotov cocktails and graffiti to damage and destroy a car lot of SUVs.

(1)

The detritus. Aftermath.
The white of containers, emptied,
telltale globs of oil, the rest ingested.
Criminals. The kind who eat candy
and leave trails of their delights,
but mostly their desires. A criminal
law book on the shelf might not seem
so incriminating next to mathematics
texts, especially in a student's room.
Silent as a tomb, caution tape
holding the scene tight,
remainders of physics and/or revenge
invisible.

They're just *kids*, this is
graduate work, and this is just
a reporter who happens upon a scene,
then carefully whispers his findings
to his audience, not realizing there is one,
maybe two, *alright,*
ten of us, and more
quietly folding the paper half by half, humming,
silently urging some kind of heroes along.

(2)

(=)
A search of the room turned up mathematical equations on a legal pad,
two full boxes of candy, take-out remains, criminal law and mathematics
texts neatly and responsibly arranged on a shelf. The life of a graduate
student: unhealthy food, pile of books, the body of a room, playing of

54

physics on a grand yellow legal pad stage. There are no pamphlets announcing political affiliations, no matchbooks, no evidence present to promote a sense of unwieldiness. It is just so. The reporter tells it like he sees it, we read, our fingers turn black from newsprint and we make mental notes for ourselves, the future crime scenes we might leave behind.

( )

Not a shack in the woods: this is the inner layer. Students of well-known graduate programs, larvae of a sort, but bursting like the infernos they allegedly set. Notebooks with code of mathematics your average newspaper reader might not get. The equations stick out their feet and laugh off the page. These students are candy-eaters who order take-out, set fires in their spare time. They violate metal ingenuity, let the fires eat the mind's internal combustion systems. The juries will be devoid of the likes of us; the black robes won't harness our hot bodies. Cameras and computers point their digital fingers, and the fingers that once keystroked admissions of responsibility leave a guiltless fingerprint on the body, this room.

Wendy C. Ortiz

The Women in My Family

preach dark,
deep, grow knots of worry
like gnarled tree trunks

then wail
when the wildfires come.
They are the most bitter

coffee without the cream
and no money for sugar.
We drink bitter together,

these women and I,
who harbor uncharted
territory and numerous moons

that sometimes frighten
and confuse us.
With each new woman, the maps

are transformed: the oceans,
the valley, plateaus
reveal themselves

here

in the pages that come
from my hands,
bloody and warm from the dark,
wet and fragrant from the deep.

AMBER TAMBLYN

Quentin Dean

Was last seen in the last scene
of *A Person Unknown*.

Could be overheard offering lasso lessons
to the mortician on his day off.

Kept a box of Black Widow Spiders as pets.
Fed them fresh aphids from the bellies of Calla Lilies.

Once poured a bottle of Compari in the kiddy pool,
dared Patrick to dive.

Broke my brother's heart
like the shell of an egg between meals.

Never spoke of it again.

Insisted we make the soup from scratch.

Told us if we wanted to fly in our dreams
we must eat cayenne pepper before bed.

Had a doppelganger in Nebraska
who sketched missing horses for a living.

Took too many mushrooms one summer, spent an afternoon reading
Scripture and Meisner leaning over
an ice tray in the freezer.

Sent a care package of Bologna packed with frozen books.

Sent all the historians thank you notes on stationary
baring their mothers' names.

Sent her biographer to a mental institution.

Kissed me in a neon alley in fake Paris.

In between Russian Roulette's bullets.

All up against the fortune teller's window.

Walked the walk.
Talked the dirty talk.

Tongue-tied the sword-swallower,
made a cherry stem out of him.

Never tied the knot.

Had four children.
Was survived by three children.

Went by the name, "Andrea."

Was also known as "Palmer."

Will be remembered as "Delores."

A.k.a. "Corky."

Gave me the nickname "Blue Kid."

Is still alive.

Never lived.

UNTITLED ACTRESS

Submission calls for an actress mid to late 20's. All ethnicities acceptable. Except Asian American. Caucasian preferable. Must read teen on screen. Thin but not gaunt. Lean. Quirky but not unattractive. No brown eyes. Not taller than 5'5." Weight no more than 109. Actress should have great smile. Straight teeth a must. Must be flexible. Small bust a plus. Can do own stunts. Will waive rights to image, likeness, publicity and final cut.

Role calls for nudity. Role calls for simulated sexual intercourse. Role calls for role play with lead male. No stand-in avail. Role pays scale.

Character is shy yet co-dependent, searching for love in all the wrong men. Character confides in others at her own risk. Character suffers from self doubt, a sense of worthlessness, fatigued, hollow. Character learns the hard way to believe in herself. No brown eyes. Character finally finds happiness when she meets Brad, a successful older businessman, 5'5."

Logline: A woman fights to save her soul. Think a young Carol Lombard meets a younger Anna Nicole. Requires an actress that will leave an audience speechless, whose found her creative voice. Not a speaking role.

LYNNE THOMPSON

The Unworshipped Woman

Nothing
        beat her

Break her down or   reek so
       the way she do

Nothing got her unzipped mind
       her flypaper memory

She a riverbed   will be
for a dog's millennium

        She gone lost
to her unborns   she pale smoke

Shadow   in the distance

     She a train whistler's whistle

 This unworshipped   this   woman

She come like salt lick   she go down
like a drowning man hollering for one last last

Her story hung like seaweed
     She come in   She go out

Like unworshipped women   supposed to

Knees bloody
          knuckles got somebody's
jawbone jammed on

     Hair coiled with September twatterlight
    corkscrewed so tight even owls won't hoot

until   she pass by them   longing, on long legs

Lynne Thompson

    lips the color of peril
Bittersweet folded round a hollow in her twisted back

    but   her one good eye   *it flash!*—

Song for Two Immigrants

I thought I knew you. To me, you were the Grenadines,
the Anglican Church, and a cricket match every Sunday
and every Sunday, you were Fort Charlotte, the Vincy Mas,
and blue tide pools. You were Arawaks sailing into Kingstown
Harbor. You were English and French patois, rainforests,
regatta and a Congo snake, whelk, *rotis,* lobster, and rum.

Yet, here you are in a yellowing photograph, in the Mojave or
Death Valley, CA, looking like deserters from an American war:
her every bit the boy, hair slicked, leather jacket cinched at her
throat, her tiny foot on the running board of a black '37 Ford
coupé and you, looking nothing less than the black Clyde Barrow,
flicking the butt of your Lucky Strike, checking out your boys
at play in the dirt, wearing short pants and high-tops—everyone
looking for all the world as if the Caribbean was a dream, a far
yesterday away—and it was, and it's clear: I did not know you.

Lynne Thompson

Laceum

Inspired by a photo of Camila Rocha's
tattooed torso on display at the Craft &
Folk Arts Museum, L.A

Whenever he thinks of me (*he will*), he will
think of me walking away, my body turned
against another weariness, my hips inked with
roses and he'll be convinced he can smell them,
each petal wafting its singular fragrant particular,
its own design, and he will believe that when
he saw me last, I was clothed in only blue lace,
blue as blue as the harbor at Toulon, pale blue,
forget-me-blue, blueberry, blue of the high-stepping
Prussians, of ice, of hard boys, the politics of scratch,
Egyptian blue ground from silica, copper and lime,
the indigo described by Pliny the Elder, the blue
of the cloak of Christ in the Hagia Sophia,
in the pottery at Delft or Van Gogh's *Starry Night.*
And when he recalls the lace (from the vulgar
Latin: *laceum*)—linen or silk, purl-knitted table-
cloth or doily for wounded flesh—then he will recall
that I was adorned with ribbons colored pink, *gulabi,*
cherry blossom, *rosa,* flamingo and Amazon dolphin.
Also our sorrow: I never stopped or turned around.

Red Jasper

Swift Coronas and vintage Mercedes-Benzes serenade—piston strumming piston—as they cruise Highway 134. Radios blare the twin *talk-talk* of the born again and arena football. James the Godfather croons *this is a man's world* for the lady boomers who still believe it as they veer south onto the 5, skirt Chavez Ravine (and every displaced Ruiz, Ramos & Rodriguez) built into fields of faux diamonds for every boy who prays to play past summer. Every driver slows for the cops or eighteen-wheelers, loops the River Los Angeles with its confessions buried in concrete under a stubborn scent of smog, last bloom of jacarandas, and can't-squeeze-a-drop-of-rain-until-tomorrow. Some of us turn north onto the 110 and head for our weekend so there's simply no reason for all this horsepower to come to such a hard stop just south of the *arroyo seco* except that yesterday, minutes fell back into the groove they came from and today, rush hour finds itself shrouded in a dark so black all we can see in the early November sky is a hunter's moon, that orange-red gem, that highwayman gathering up our lost seasons.

BILL HICKOK

How to Get to Heaven

Take the 10
to the 405
take the 405
South to the 90
take the 90 East
to Sepulveda
take Sepulveda North
to Palms
turn Left
third house on the right
pink with green shutters
pull in the driveway
look up
put on your wings
she's waiting for you

Bill Hickok

Mahler and Me

Listening to Mahler
I hear the summer's rolling
thunder. My old man
used to say thunder was
angels bowling.
Mahler was a great composer
and I wouldn't mind having
him on my bowling team.
Ball at eye level he would
knock down the piccolos
with their chirps of cheer,
next the flutes and their
high-pitched reverie.
Down go the violins,
so spicy sweet.
Tall stand the bassoons
and oboes of woe.
Bass fiddles, French horns,
keep the ball rolling
with the dirge of shallow
thunder. The lane echoes
the maple tree's heart,
somber notes cling
to the sadness
of the chilling winds.
The cymbals come crashing
as lightning startles the air.
At last the tiny triangle
pings of salvation. And now
comes the rain, harsh.

DANA GIOIA

Cruising with the Beach Boys

So strange to hear that song again tonight
Travelling on business in a rented car,
Miles from anywhere I've been before.
And now a tune I haven't heard for years
Probably not since it last left the charts
Back in L.A. in 1969.
I can't believe I know the words by heart
And can't think of a girl to blame them on.

Every lovesick summer has its song,
And this one I pretended to despise,
But if I were alone when it came on,
I turned it up full-blast to sing along—
A primal scream in croaky baritone,
The notes all flat, the lyrics mostly slurred.
No wonder I spent so much time alone,
Making the rounds in Dad's old Thunderbird.

Some nights I drove down to the beach to park
And walk along the railings of the pier.
The water down below was cold and dark,
The waves monotonous against the shore.
The darkness and the mist, the midnight sea,
The flickering lights reflected from the city—
A perfect setting for a boy like me,
The Cecil B. DeMille of my self-pity.

I thought by now I'd left those nights behind,
Lost like the girls that I could never get,
Gone with the years, junked with the old T-Bird.
But one old song, a stretch of empty road,
Can open up a door and let them fall
Tumbling like boxes from a dusty shelf,
Tightening my throat for no reason at all,
Bringing on tears shed only for myself.

Dana Gioia

Planting a Sequoia

All afternoon my brothers and I have worked in the orchard,
Digging this hole, laying you into it, carefully packing the soil.
Rain blackened the horizon, but cold winds kept it over the Pacific,
And the sky above us stayed the dull gray
Of an old year coming to an end.

In Sicily a father plants a tree to celebrate his first son's birth—
An olive or a fig tree—a sign that the earth has one more life to bear.
I would have done the same, proudly laying new stock into my father's
    orchard,
A green sapling rising among the twisted apple boughs,
A promise of new fruit in other autumns.

But today we kneel in the cold planting you, our native giant,
Defying the practical custom of our fathers,
Wrapping in your roots a lock of hair, a piece of an infant's birth cord,
All that remains above earth of a first-born son,
A few stray atoms brought back to the elements.

We will give you what we can—our labor and our soil,
Water drawn from the earth when the skies fail,
Nights scented with the ocean fog, days softened by the circuit of bees.
We plant you in the corner of the grove, bathed in western light,
A slender shoot against the sunset.

And when our family is no more, all of his unborn brothers dead,
Every niece and nephew scattered, the house torn down,
His mother's beauty ashes in the air,
I want you to stand among strangers, all young and ephemeral to you,
Silently keeping the secret of your birth.

Dana Gioia

The Letter

And in the end, all that is really left
Is a feeling—strong and unavoidable—
That somehow we deserved something better.
That somewhere along the line things
Got fouled up. And that letter from whoever's
In charge, which certainly would have set
Everything straight between us and the world,
Never reached us. Got lost somewhere.
Possibly mislaid in some provincial station.
Or sent by mistake to an old address
Whose new tenant put it on her dresser
With the curlers and the hairspray forgetting
To give it to the landlord to forward.
And we still wait like children who have sent
Two weeks' allowance far away
To answer an enticing advertisement
From a crumbling, yellow magazine,
Watching through years as long as a childhood summer,
Checking the postbox with impatient faith,
Even on days when mail is never brought.

Dana Gioia

Money

> *Money is a kind of poetry.*
> — Wallace Stevens

Money, the long green,
cash, stash, rhino, jack
or just plain dough.

Chock it up, fork it over,
shell it out. Watch it
burn holes through pockets.

To be made of it! To have it
to burn! Greenbacks, double eagles,
megabucks and Ginnie Maes.

It greases the palm, feathers a nest,
holds heads above water,
makes both ends meet.

Money breeds money.
Gathering interest, compounding daily.
Always in circulation.

Money. You don't know where it's been,
but you put it where your mouth is.
And it talks.

SUZANNE LUMMIS

Gone, Baby

O Best Beloved, they're true, those tales
    come down to us from Way
Then. In The Age of Money the money
    vanished—overnight it did, as if
vacuumed through a funnel into deep space.
    No one had it, the money. It didn't stew
in a bank or go forth and multiply.
    Buried in the yard of the mad man it was not,
nor bent into wads and stuffed
    in the robber's pocket. It had not burned,
had not melted; no guttering molecules slid
    back to earth, their nuclei hot and
circling the memory of money.
    O Best, it went Gone. It went Ain't. It went
as if it had not been, as if our lives
    had been nothing but dreamt things
and we weren't even the primary dreamers.
    Beloved, now dream again. It's late.
Close your eyes and think of that enchanted time
    when money flowed from our palms like
blood through our veins. Then dream
    of The Age Before That, when we had only
to point and golden fruit dropped
    to our hands. And the most ancient
of all realms, imagine: The Era of Wands.
    We waved them and, Lo, it appeared—
whatever we longed for.
    And we never went hungry yet, somehow,
we always felt hunger, for there was always
    more where that came from, and always
we wanted more.

Suzanne Lummis

Street Dumb

Between the firehouse and hospital
my place—eleven seven five—
hangs above the mini-mart. All night
sirens bleet *someone's left alive*
or *someone's not quite killed.* Red
lights, whirly-gig and thrilled,
freezy hot, feed their urgencies
to the dark. But blood
on asphalt under streetlight
isn't red, it's almost black—
like someone smudged
the guy's cut-out silhouette.
No, that's a lie—scrap that.
Shadow exited a rip
so small I couldn't put it back.
No, oil thinned by shadow
drizzled from a tank.
No. I saw a man die but didn't get
shook up. I just went stupid. Blank.
So even when they said, "Well
he won't have to pay his rent,"
pulled the sheet across his face,
closed it—a long
letter no one sent—I was *huuh?*
like *duh!* like I didn't even know
what that meant.

DOUGLAS KEARNEY

City of Searchlights and Dead Cats

blocks below us, the searchlights
bend, street lines into descent—

the Ghetto Bird makes its vulture round—
a muzzle flash up and down

somewhere a block away, someone breaks,
running for a ride. the cops roll up

and down the blocks below us.
we bend into descent.

and what to call the homie now,
the name I cried at the ivy whip—

leaves the shape of vipers' skulls
leaves his hands stripped—no longer fits.

don't play up in that ivy, y'all
there're snakes in all the vines. the lines

of his name became the drawl of red aerosol.
a language you taught me. a bullet makes

a mouth in a heart, a toothless mouth. the bones
a handful of dominoes.

call him "Buph Loc," nigga, the mouth says,
at once a tilted 40.

***FEVER!* the bones buried in the card table. i**
empty my wallet of cusswords. *domino!*

Douglas Kearney

I can't seem to beat you. I hold my bones,
their dull eyes gawking black at me.

Dallas!
brother!

you stared down a coyote.
you snuck home a kitten.

I am letting my bones drop,
a wall unbuilding. I stare

at each eye, slowly counting.
you know, now, I walk every street

I ever walk knowing how I'd kill
everyone I've come across?

and when I look at you, I am gawking back
at me, needing new eyes.

and when i looked at my boys,
they became a gang just as 1-time

suspected. and when my boys turned on me,
school was a mess of ivy.

those nights, coyotes in scared packs
upset cans to get at the sacks

of cold cuts gone bad, take-home chicken bones.
those nights, I ran ammonia over the remains,

those sour nights sliced by copter blades.
the possums and their buckshot eyes

Douglas Kearney

taught us to lay dead, as suspected.
my name X'd off the walls; still

my posse never fought
me. we were coyotes at heart.

they became Grimace, Dimen', Inches, Goldy:
for his skin, his hope. that was then,

I don't call them now. I don't know

what happened? pops wouldn't say.
I drive home, my headlights

break against big coyotes ambling
toward a fence. bold now,

swole from eating cats; upright trash
cans line the drives like families

awaiting those inevitable hearses. I drag
the garbage, clutch an ax handle,

trundle past where Pops found her,
mangled, the cat you brought home years ago

without permission. a muzzle flashes up
and down somewhere a block away

a coyote fills its mouth with red aerosol
and swaggers up the street.

the searchlights hit it,
new eyes glare back.

JAWANZA DUMISANI

Odell's Desire

That Odell is tight as dick's hatband.
Grips a candy red '62 drop-top Caddy
four fingers of Thunderbird boils in the glove,
his basement conk shimmers like onyx.
It's Friday; the eagle's flew,
sports white polyester
like a ticket to heaven.

Eyeing his boys grant blessings,
five turn the corner tattered
cardboard to concrete
worn soles flap rhythm he's deaf to.
Daddy, Daddy, give us some money!
Two bits flipped above straw brim's tilt
here, split it & slide as it lands
in dirty palm of 3rd eldest.

The meter's off
& it's too hot for hosiery.
Sliced from southern pride's hip
switching hard enough to churn butter
a hooker draped in cheap scarlet
leaks her dime store enchantment
down fast lane of his desire.
Hey slim goody, what them draws flop fo'?
"Twelve & three sweetie."
Here's ten in my back seat.

Miz Rodchester feels engine heat; shakes her head,
mutters prayer for those living off their hide
Ol' Lady Cobb peeks from a 2nd floor window
pressing cornstarch into a week's blue collar.

Front end swings into an alley & parks,
King Pleasure serenades her shallow touch
soothes like a phantom mother from his past.
Odell kindles his lust, divides pigeon dung
on a rusty VW, into how many strokes
the flame lasts & picks a Tri-fecta.

Daddy's Epitaph

After boot camp, Alphonso your eldest, renamed you Sir
Kool Menthol & time clocks rigged for spring

Scrawny imposters at Ford Motor, spun from sweat & steel
Cast into men mimicking each drag

Aunt Mariah brands you Congo,
Wandering crusader for lost infidels

Yang of Uncle Simon, a paisley ascot; I wonder
How long ago & which side of the Nile you roamed

We are both distant twins of antiquity
Boxed in 3 by 6 pantry we dance the ceremony of anger

Yo' captoe, ham-boned into my hide
Love's unspoken invocation, not a broke dish

Baptized in maid's water, I dip these hands to save you
Wash your back, bow my head & pray

Your hand serves righteous discipline
Mine reserved to dignify you

I, 3rd son of blue hurricanes
You, forgotten dynasty of tongues

Architect of my breath
These palms keloid in reverence

Son of an emancipated sharecropper,
Pinned two days inside a mine in West Virginia

Crushed shoulders, coiled spine
Fallen parishioner, gutted by black lung, dragged

Each holy morning; Royal Crown Pomade,
A stocking cap & one tarnished penny crowns you king

Jawanza Dumisani

I dreaded Sabbath 'til you
Passed out five pennies for the plate

Rev. Perkins swore by a snake in the garden
Secret sentry at door of infidelity

Truth revealed by a close cousin
Only dialect we own

You begged forgiveness from 7th pew for little more
Greater treasures retrieved from your Naugahyde rocking chair

You & Mother anchor a sea of sepia
East mantel an archway

Of our brick two-family flat off West Grade River
Plastic slipcovers, McDonald's first Friday & no garage

Powder blue Fairlane rusting in our driveway,
Relic of your phosphorus glow

Last breath stuck in my throat
Ushering earth to swallow you whole

LORY BEDIKIAN

Driveways

I never understood the appeal of it:
sofa pushed to one side of the concrete
rectangle, dented garbage cans on the other,
a pistachio-colored carport over the top.

We could hear the growl
of motorcycles as they crept back
onto sidewalks until their silver bodies
blurred and then, a tunnel of noise.

Twelve, content with a borrowed bike,
I rode up and down blocks observing
the long tongues of asphalt
or white-gray stone stretched into

the runways of our suburban bungalows.
I never made sense of parked boats
covered with blue tarps, secured
from some imaginary wind, dry,

except for the occasional sprinkler
teasing its starboard side. The way
people haggled on these stretches,
washed their oil-stained squares

clean with soap, took a smoke
on a beach chair or simply stood,
hands on hips, staring toward nothing,
thinking of a time long since passed,

baffled me. The roads deserted—
now and then a pick-up truck
buzzing by, the mailman's blue bag
flashing over the concrete's bare back.

Lory Bedikian

Children used them best.
Cracks were rivers, their tricycles
trains, or the slab became an island,
a basketball court, a jungle or long-awaited

classroom. It was the same square on which
they left for college, for marriage,
for some reason—and if the reasons weren't clear,
other driveways buzzed with the possibilities.

And some families fought on them—
boxing rings with someone on the lower
corner, ready to exit to sidewalk, to car,
leaving but never for good. The one standing

on the upper side, left to garden,
pulling weeds like hair, raking as if they'd find
an X somewhere, finally revealing how to get
out of this place. Front yard abandoned,

after dusk, two headlights drag
through the dark, below plum trees.
Driveways were our altars, where we could bless
and curse what we became. I rode home,

too small to know that something
makes us want to see the world
from this vantage point, from ground hardened
over earth, blaring with noonday sun,

a dead flag under our feet, rolled out
to claim a plot of land, feeling the movement
of years upon it, hand over the eyes,
calling to the window above.

Lory Bedikian

The Mechanic

Stretching over the carburetor,
he shouts about the quality of life here
compared to back home, how they stood
in line for bread, how there were no cedars
more green than those by the shore.

He could be my uncle in Syria, 1948,
a man taking in fumes, a cigarette balancing
on a fender, hands lined with grease,
saving coins in a jar for his newborn,
losing relatives to malaria, to civil war.

But today we're in Hollywood—the palms
dry. This man speaks to me in Armenian.
He remembers working late into the Lebanese night,
the plaza's noise of backgammon boards,
headlights beaming beyond the Mediterranean.

Now, he's used to customers calling out
his American nickname, while he wrenches
spark plugs into place, the old country
preserved on a calendar. He's used to this
new world of dollar bills, available parts.

I say bless him and this hand-made auto shop,
the first opening, closing of hoods, pump of pistons.
And bless the one who never made it over
the Atlantic, an arm extending into the engine,
a scar exposed, the shape of an eagle's wing.

HENRY J. MORRO

Any Job

The men straggle into the cold warehouse
draped in tattered shirts, torn sweaters,
army jackets, their hats crowned
with logos—NY Yankees, UCLA,
Puerto Rico. Sometimes when they speak
I see gaping holes in their mouths
from the missing teeth.
Sometimes they arrive
in twos or threes—wandering
from warehouse to warehouse like a lost tribe.
Sometimes a son will lead his father
and speak for him, the father standing back,
his eyes wide open, the son boasting to me,
He can drive anything...give him a shot.
When they fill out the applications,
they scribble the reason
for leaving each job:
laid off
temp work only
company moved away
owner died
Sometimes one of them is bold
enough to write *fired.*
Another one wrote,
fired for fighting,
and for another job he wrote,
fired for drinking with the boss.
Under "Special Skills" they scrawl:
forklift
spanish
typing
sweeping
I glance out the window
at the downtown skyline.
I know that when I pull down
the *Help Wanted* sign they will still keep
shuffling into the warehouse,
hunched in the cold,
gaping holes in their mouths.

Henry J. Morro

Three Generations of Loving Marilyn

I'm fuzzy on how I came to love her,
but when Dad uttered *It's Marilyn*—
we swept into the living room
to watch *Some Like it Hot*
on the black and white TV.
She reigned on the screen
with her sexy sway, as if her knees
were tethered together
by a fine leather braid.

It was Dad's impulse to pause
the family for everything Marilyn—pointing
to her *Gentlemen Prefer Blondes* poster
on the side of the bus or
holding up a Marilyn lamp shade
at Woolworth and proposing
for the dining room?

Yesterday, wearing white sunglasses,
and a Marilyn rhinestone T-shirt,
my teen-age daughter sauntered
down the stairs out to the family BBQ.
Pivoting in the sun,
she watched two seagulls fly
towards the ocean—
then she raised her chilled wine,
took a sip
and entered summer.

Henry J. Morro

The Boxing Shrine

—for Benny Kid Paret, 1937-1962
Welterweight Champion

When we hunkered down on the sofa to watch Sugar Ray,
my dad worshiped how he could dance and hit a man
at the same time, and when Robinson closed in for the finish,
he'd jump up fisting the air—*Deck him! Deck him!*

After a good fight, he and his brothers would re-enact
the bruising highlights—a right cross, a left hook, an upper cut,
boom...an uncle would drop. Even in their scrawny bodies
my uncles thought they were tough, bobbing and weaving
their silly pompadours.

During the Welterweight Championship bout,
New York, 1962, Emile Griffith trapped Benny Kid Paret
against the ropes in the twelfth round,
and pounded his skull with his iron fists, 29 punches in a row,
the Kid hanging, his head a sack of bones.

It was the brawl my uncles dreamed of until the Kid collapsed
onto the canvas, his mouthpiece lying next to his bulging eye.
Lifting the Kid out of the ring high on a stretcher,
the paramedics wedged through the fans.

For ten days the Kid floated in a coma surrounded by candles,
the click of rosary beads sliding through fingers.
For ten days the former sugar cane cutter lay half-dead
as mourners journeyed to his bed, offering bouquets and crucifixes
in their tender hands, petals crushed on the floor.

After they buried Benny Kid Paret, I knelt in front of the TV.
In the flickering snow I could see the ghost in the ring,
his muscular arms pressed against the bloody ropes.
I wandered to the stairs, leaned my head against the wooden rails.
Through the open window, I heard the streetcar—
my uncles bobbing and weaving in the night.

MAJID NAFICY

Chess

Near Santa Monica Pier
There is a checkered sign
With eight wooden tables.
It is raining today.
The waves reach the boardwalk
Playing with the wooden legs
And the sand has covered the tabletop.
I count... four seagulls sitting
On the edge of the last table,
Looking toward the water.

I was nine years old
When I learned to play chess.
My first set came in a red box
With golden margins on the top
And little black and white chessmen
Pinned into the checkered board
And two empty spots for the dead.
It was a gift from my cousin
We were at their house in Tehran.
They had spread Persian carpets
On wooden sofas in the backyard
The scent of citron was in the air
Mostafa was hosing the hot bricks
My mother was dangling her legs in the pool
And my uncle was doing his evening prayer
Facing the colorful flowers and hedges
Mehdy and I were lying on our bellies,
Playing chess in dim light.

The rain has stopped
But the wind is still playing
With the sand on the tables.
And I am looking at the seagulls
They have long, slender legs
Like my first, little chessmen.

Hope

Emily Dickinson calls "hope" a bird
Who has perched in her soul
And without asking for seeds
Sings incessantly.

I saw it as a cricket
Who appeared in my childhood dreams,
Grew in my adolescent poems
And disappeared in the hubbub of a revolution.

Today I am left alone in exile
And yet, when I go to the balcony
To water the only flower in my house,
I hear the sound of a cricket
Who is calling me
From behind my neighbor's bamboos.

YVONNE M. ESTRADA

Johnny Doe

Policemen pose like plastic toy soldiers,
point rifle barrels in every direction;
ghetto bird's spotlight glints off helmets.
Ambulance allowed across yellow tape,
diesel engine grinds up the sharp grade.
In no moon you glow, fish white belly up,
streetlamp casts mottled shadows,
your blood a preschool finger painting
smeared on sidewalk.
I am ordered to shear off your slick, soaked
jeans, to smash your chest, beat your heart
for you. Your arms extend savior-like,
needles pounded into veins,
translucent bags held skyward
like offerings to a life giving deity;
clear liquid bleeds in, your blood pours out,
three bullet holes versus six-minute
trip to emergency room.
How old are you?
I think about my son asleep at home.
I wonder if *your* mother's at work.
I breathe deep, drive fast,
make the siren a prayer
too loud for your God to ignore.

Yvonne M. Estrada

A Fresh Coat of Night

A fresh coat of night ends another day.
One bored boy sees no one in the mirror,
shaves his head 'til he's a perfect cliché
homeboy artist starting a new career
fills sagged stained jeans with aerosol colors,
slams the screen door, crunches across dry lawns,
complete faith in apathetic neighbors
in their white bubbles of television.
Past Target, the church. and little league teams,
Button finger twitches impatiently,
like a dog's leg while she dreams.
He is a blue mist sprayed in an alley,
wet paint drips, weeps proof this is his scrawled world,
the image attached to something solid.

String Theory No Joke

A string walks into a bar.
A huge crowd has gathered.
Before him the bartender
places a plastic red basket
of hot wings and cheese toast.
The string breathes in, then sighs,
blesses the food.
Cocktail waitresses pass it out.
Even the hecklers eat,
they taunt the string,
they sneer,
"If you come from the cosmic net,
then weave us a miracle,
a blanket that brings back the dead,
or fly a kite into the parallel universe.
Here, take these soup cans,
stretch yourself between them,
take one to heaven,
set the other one on the bar
so we can listen
to the voice of God."

SHERMAN PEARL

Salvation in the Dead Zone

In the desert of the dead zone
you lose contact with big city stations,
the babble of news, commercials
promising that whatever you need
is a phone call away.
In the dead zone there's no one to call.
The car's antenna bends backward
to catch the last waves
of what you've left behind.
From the invisible noontime moon
you get strains of country/western
on the only band still audible.
These songs of loss
are what you came for, anthems
of a land that's breaking your heart.
They wail about love
that was killed by the sun and left half-
buried in sand.
Your car crawls from mirage to mirage
till the guitars plunk out
and radio's playing nothing
but static, the crackle of desolation.
You drove all this way
for solitude and it terrifies you.
You listen a while
to the rasp that sounds like a signal
from some distant galaxy
then twist the dial
like a gambler betting everything
on his last toss of dice.
A faint voice comes through the haze,
some snake-oil preacher
hissing about Jesus and life ever-lasting.
You turn up the volume.

Sherman Pearl

What I Came For

flashed at me, called out from the kitchen
and the instant I reached for it
vanished—poof—filled my hand with its absence,
my mind with its shadows.

I looked for it in the fridge, stood in the chilly light
nibbling leftovers, testing for the taste
of whatever it was I'd come for.
I rummaged for it in drawers full of nameless gadgets;
I scanned the cabinets, searched the bowls,
emptied teacups for clues

and wondered if what I came for
was in the bedroom, maybe, under blankets
where my wife and I find each other, solid and warm,

or in the bathroom where odors thick with memory
might lead me snuffling like a bloodhound
to the thing I've come for.
I followed my footsteps
through deep pile carpeting, found traces
of what I dropped on the way but not what I came for.

What I came for buzzes my hair, tingles my veins;
it churns in me
when I add up my blessings and discover one missing.

One night I'll find it. I'll be at the table with my wife
having late supper, chewing the day.
I'll bite into something tangy and foreign she's cooked
or look up at the wall clock, surprised at the hour
and it will come to me.

I'll savor it, swallow it, feel its downward passage.
We'll laugh about things we've lost in the air.
We'll say *Look what we've come to.*

GLORIA VANDO

My 90-Year-Old Father and My Husband Discuss Their Trips to the Moon

—for Bill

On the balcony I hear my father
speak of craters, their depth, their breadth;
how he measured his lunar steps so as not to falter,

sidestepping their cavernous mouths to peer in,
his echo resounding in their hearts.
He was on the moon's good side, the one

that smiles and on occasion winks at earth.
With audible pride, he explains he was the lone
civilian on the mission. Yet he was happy to come home.

Yes, my husband says, *it was wonderful for me too!
Shepard led me by the hand around the rim
of Eratosthenes.* My father laughs at the similarity

of the crater's name to his own, Erasmus.
He is glad Bill understands him,
relieved someone else knows how desolate it can be

out there. *Not only desolate*, Bill says,
putting an arm around my father's frail shoulders,
I also know how lonely it can get.

Gloria Vando

He2-104: A True Planetary Nebula in the Making

On the universal clock, Sagan tells us,
we are only moments old. And this
new crab-like discovery in Centaurus,
though older by far, is but
an adolescent going through a vital
if brief stage in the evolution
of interacting stars. I see it
starting its sidereal trek
through midlife, glowingly complex—
"a pulsating red giant" with a "small
hot companion" in tow—and think
of you and me that night in August
speeding across Texas in your red
Mustang convertible, enveloped in dust
and fumes, aiming for a motel bed,
settling instead for the backseat of the car,
arms and legs flailing in all directions,
but mostly toward heaven—and now
this cool red dude winking at me
through the centuries as if to say
I know, I know, sidling in closer
to his sidekick, shedding his garments,
shaking off dust, encircling
her small girth with a high-density
lasso of himself, high-velocity
sparks shooting from her ringed
body like crazy legs and arms until
at last, he's got his hot companion
in a classic hold and slowly,
in ecstasy, they take wing and
blaze as one across the Southern skies—
no longer crab but butterfly.

DOUG KNOTT

"Last of the Knotts"
—Selection from One Man Show

(Narrator+Carolyn) "We meet at the old Schwab's counter"

We met at the old Schwab's drug store on Sunset just before it
closed for good, when this waitress that I knew, Irene, with the ironed-
up hair, actually introduced us at the counter, where we were sitting side
by side. "You two should really meet each other."

So we did. It was easy because we had history. We'd lived within a
few blocks of each other in San Francisco, and so could walk the same
streets and talk the same shops in our minds. We'd come to LA to start
over... and found each other. We swam together like long-necked swans.

Carolyn was so beautiful it made me cringe. She was tall and slender,
with black hair spiked out like a coconut palm. Her face was a medallion
of blue eyes, and her skin was warm and soft like a fresh glazed donut.
We had a lot in common: music, cigarettes, coffee, late-night clubs,
cocaine... and sex.

At the end of our second date, when I knew we were on our way to
bed, I said, "Maybe you'd like to try this.".. and hauled out my little
brown vial of cocaine. She said, "Why don't you try this?' and brought
out her big stash—because it turned out, she was actually... a dealer.
But very above-board, clean and genteel, and only to four regular clients.
It was to fund her dream of making expensive hip clothing out of old
burlap bags. No joke: so you could see the shaggy seams, and the labels,
and how the garment is made, right on the surface of it. And she was
good at it.

All this meant I fell in love with her like a charmed goat.

ROBERT MEZEY

Please?

If I swung through the jungle on a vine
And beat my chest, impatient to entwine,
Or else came on more civilized, more benign,
And knelt down at your feet or lay supine,
Making vague gestures, an ambiguous sign
Towards the general area of your shrine,
As if suggesting that you too recline,
Or even if I, by accident or design,
Let slip that love is but an anodyne,
A temporary balm, however fine,
Yes, even if I should all love resign
And let my hair grow long and swear off wine
And never write another goddamn line,
Darling, wouldn't you be my Valentine?

LINDA ALBERTANO

Beloved

Thou art incendiary.
Thou sendest me up in sparks
                    100 times a day.
Thou makest me hum like 1000
            buzzing phone lines yammering through
                    dizzy night.

When thou smilest upon me, I'm
            money in the bank.
When thou snarlest, I am as a bad
            check, bounced, and cowering
            in thy heart's darkest dumpster.

Thou art the Lion of La Cienega,
            the Rose of Sherman Way.
            I love to lay eyes on thee.

Thou ringest through me sudden
            and bright as fresh champagne.
My switchboard overloadeth.

Thy breath is as clean laundry
            folded behind thy lips.
Thy teeth art as white Lincolns
            parked in neat rows.

I love to taste the texture
            of thy skin.
Thine eyes art interstellar.

Beloved,
            thou art incendiary.

Thou sendest me up in sparks!

S.A. GRIFFIN

I Choose Not to Believe in War Holy or Not

if I were Christ I would be a drink of water
if I were Buddha I would gladly kill myself
    in the garden of your eyes forever
if I were Mohammed Mecca would be the journey in your touch
if I were a Jew the holy land would be the covenant of my blood
    singing hosanna in your veins
if I were an atheist I would call your every footfall god leaving
    footprints in the moment

ALEXIS RHONE FANCHER

the seven stages of love—an l.a. haiku-noir sequence

the lure
bring your tender love
to the city, 8th floor, the
door's ajar. find me!

the operating instructions
she explicitly
told me how to please her, but
then, she always lied.

the truth
as she walked away
she said, yes, I love women.

I just don't love you.

the rationalization
life's cruel casting call:
I can play taller, blonder,
but I can't play you.

the big missing
if matter cannot
be created or destroyed,
is she still out there?

the acceptance
so tired tonight. you'd
think the bottom had dropped out
of my intentions.

the bullet dodged
deep in my breathing
I stand outside of myself
and see me, breathing.

CHARLOTTE INNES

The Ex

"Did you love him?" my friend asked, as I mowed the lawn.
I stopped, surveyed the shredded grass for a moment, torn
between what I believed was true and what I thought
might be. I wasn't sure. "Well?" "I think I bought
a story. I mean *we* did. God, it seemed—" "Go on."

He turned the radio off. Peace! All summer long,
we'd listened to unrelenting Olympic cheer from dawn
to dusk, while all my thoughts had wrestled down the fraught
      "did-you-love-him"

question. Crushing "yes!" Spitting "no!" That it was "wrong"
to want to call—though just to help us both move on,
of course. My friend began to carve the lamb. "You'll sort
it out. Let's eat." "But the lawn…" "…can wait. Look, I've brought
your favorite wine." And the full moon rising seemed to yawn,
      "Did you love him?"

ROLLAND VASIN
(aka Vachine)

Yama

A new light bathes my torso, nimble gentle fingers caress my limbs,
coos as soft as a turtledove's breast fill places I forgot were empty.

Lips the nutty flavor of sweet cream and bitter tea in the morning, her
face a Weather Channel report on the climate along destiny's highway.

A Hippie at core, hair dye masks those silver strands that blow her cover,
God damn, have I fallen in love? A reservist called out to serve again?

HARRY E. NORTHUP

Make a Poem

Make a poem from pavement, fragmented & black, uneven,
broken.

Make a poem from an experience, memory, grief.
Make an email a poem.
Make a poem from tweets, write it at intervals,
over a day.

Make a poem from death & hunger.
Make a poem out of embracing a fear.
Make a poem out of wanting to tell someone something.
Make a poem out of fear, vulnerability, poverty of spirit.

Make a poem from poems that you've read.
Poems come from poems.
Read the language school poets as well as the romantic poets.
While you struggle with learning the many forms,
learn the tradition of poetry, especially the epics.

Make a poem from tennis, sweet potatoes & ruin.
Make a poem from beauty & disgrace.
Make a poem from bowing down to a greater craftsman.
Make a poem out of women & men & trees
with jacaranda blossoms fallen on the sidewalk.
Make a poem from hills & viaduct & sod houses &
country roads & a 2 story red brick schoolhouse.
Out of pride & discounted emotions, make a poem at evening.

Traffic Both Ways on Prospect

What do you say to a fellow poet in prison?
Practice the *imagistes* rules:
"1. Direct treatment of the 'thing,' whether
subjective or objective.
2. To use absolutely no word that did not
contribute to the presentation.
3. As regarding rhythm: to compose in sequence
of the musical phrase, not in sequence of a metronome."
Or tell him to read Wordsworth's The Prelude...
Or Pound's section about character in The Cantos.

When I was in my deepest sorrow, I read the poems
of St. John of the Cross, later the poems of Rilke.
Or I've read The Bible out loud & to myself.
I'm okay as long as I am with some one.
Walks in the city give me solace.

I was sitting at Starbucks on the NW corner of Vermont
& Prospect last night & I thought about you.
I was eating a cup of caramel ice cream as I was watching
the traffic going north & south on Vermont, the cars
& motorcycles going east & west on Hollywood &
I thought about you.

I remember seeing you at this Starbucks & we talked.
The solace of the night holds freedom lost.

SESSHU FOSTER

Movie Version: "Hell to Eternity"

Guy Gabaldon, born in 1926 and raised in East L.A., shined shoes on skid row from the age of ten. At twelve, he moved in with the Nakano family of Boyle Heights, where he learned Japanese. When the Nakanos were sent to camps in Arizona, 17 year old Gabaldon joined the marines and used "backstreet Japanese" to capture 1,500 Japanese troops on Saipan. In the movie version, he was played by a white actor named Jeffrey Hunter, who suffered a stroke at age 42 in 1969 and died falling down the stairs.

In the movie version, skid row was played by 1960s Bunker Hill and age 12 was played by a grasshopper flying in a summer field. Sweetness careened down the streets in buses and trolleys.

In the movie version, a ten year old boy shining shoes was played by Route 66 and the relocation camps were played by cars going by. Packards were played by Dodges.

In the movie version, the cold beer is played by country music nasal twang, and Jeffrey Hunter was played by slight nausea and nostril flare. His headache was played by the 20th century.

In the movie version, the actual colors of the rushing ocean were played by a whirr of a strip through the machine and the sizzling palm leaves were played by folded taco smell. Somebody was played by nobody.

In the movie version, the present is played by an off-camera past with seagulls added or removed and palm trees painted on a canvas backdrop of night. Popcorn smell was played by cotton candy.

In the movie version, wishes were played by a voice over of broken dishes and bouts of influenza were played by old magazines in the back. Smoke in a funnel over the hills was played by extras dressed like citizens.

In the movie version, East L.A. was played by the blood bursting an artery and dust specks thrown into a ray on the stairs. The golden moment balking.

Time Studies #75

I could be riding in a truck, but the narrative was familiar, constructed of big sheets of weathered plywood, encrusted with cement, something with girls, black fabric of night, the street corner in daylight.

Usually I felt that I might retreat into my mind, but I soon realized most anyone could see in there what I was thinking, it was like an abandoned motel.

The succulent cacti swelled with information, the purplish ravine coursed over the rocks, pungent sage and mountain laurel with red berries full of small birds. It was breezy and confusing to some of us.

Her joy was so amazing it seemed to represent generations of women, both inside and outside of her family. Many wanted to feel a part of it. It marked a generation of people who passed on her street.

Some secret in the blood as if it were words, engineering, direction—something static, objective like that. Present in her voice.

Somehow we get the message that we are too late. Of course, we must go anyway, even if we are the last to know. We must go.

She invited me to go to her wedding in Vegas. I felt she might understand why I would not go. But I hoped that she'd be too busy, too happy, to even think about me.

And a thin film is brushed over the surface, as if by a deliberate hand, like the stream across smooth granite, sugar glaze across pastry dough, history across sweetness of seasons.

Sesshu Foster

Taylor's Question

—how do you survive, how do you make it through?

Always listen to the women.

My father broke my mother's nose, her hand. But he didn't die alone.
Two of my sisters were there, holding his hand.

Driving down the street you make a sudden maneuver to dodge a stalled
vehicle and the guy on your tail flips a switch when you cut him off,
speeds up and cuts in front of you, screaming and flipping you off, jams
on his brakes so his bumper comes up on your vehicle, you're swerving
out of the lane to evade, speeding to pass in the traffic on the avenue—
dusk falling—you're laughing because he speeds up, both vehicles
beginning to race; a woman's voice rises to a pitch: "No, no, no!"
And you're reluctant, but already you're slowing.

Listen.

LARRY COLKER

Mid Size Dog

- from Sigalert.com (Los Angeles), April 26, 2006

6:44 AM	110 North at 105 East Loose Animal Live Dog in Car Pool Lane
6:45 AM	Medium White/beige Dog
6:58 AM	North 110 at 105 Just South of Manchester Dog Hit in Center Divider
7:03 AM	Freeway Tow Service Patrol On Scene Will Standby for CHP
7:30 AM	Advised CHP Will Need a Snare Dog in Center Divider By Car Pool Lane
7:44 AM	Brown/white Pit Bull Still Alive, Curled Up on Center Divider
7:47 AM	Please Roll Animal Control
7:49 AM	Telephoned Animal Control, Ans Mach, Office Opens at 0800 Hrs
8:05 AM	Freeway Tow Driver on Lane l With the Dog Do U Have an ETA
8:06 AM	Freeway Tow Driver Still on Lane l Do U Have an ETA for Him
8:09 AM	CHP On Scene North 110 at 105 Dog at Center Divider Injured
8:10 AM	Advised Animal Control En Route
8:10 AM	Center Divider, Possible Fatality, Mid Size Dog

Larry Colker

Projector

Half sewing machine, half tank,
it was the closest thing I knew to a holy relic.

Elders fetched it from the closet
like the ark of our covenant with the past.

First came the ghosts of those who lie in the ground,
jerky simulacra dancing to staccato chatter.

Then came the famous line-up of the nine cousins,
four in diapers, three crying, all with chicken pox.

Then here we are, recognizable at last, in Florida,
making faces at the camera, in the background dolphins leaping.

O maker of humanity in its image,
O moving art,

you made light of us all.
We glowed.

Larry Colker

The Leap

We stood in groups of twos and threes
on the sidewalk outside the bar,
talking, smoking, watching traffic and each other,
one quiet old guy by himself looking at the moon,

when a quick motion caught our eyes
as the girl pounced onto her boyfriend,
shimmied up his tall torso,
squeezed her legs around his waist,
clasped her arms around his neck,
pressed her face into his hair.

If I were a prophet I'd say
a burst of light surrounded them
like a glory. Like revelation, like satori,
we were all converted on the spot:
for the rest of our lives we'd wait
for such a rapture, such a wrapped her,
our bodies suddenly made heavy
with bone and flesh not our own.

I caught the old man staring
dumbstruck, until he collected himself,
went back to looking at stars.

At first the boyfriend took it like a puppy's exuberance,
continued the conversation, as though that leap,
still rebounding in our chests,
was nothing special. But his girl did not unlatch,
tightened her arms and legs around him
until who knows what was let loose inside,
and he hugged her back, with a shy smile at us
as if embarrassed by his riches.

JAMIE ASAYE FITZGERALD

Presence/Absence

The jacaranda blooms
had to be bright
when the plums
fell from the branch

or the seasons
would have halted
altogether: summer,
fall, winter, spring

abandoning the rose
and bougainvillea,
the cats who once
slept in the shade.

I have read, the reaches
of love are boundless,
yet small phenomenon
have I seen—

hummingbirds enticed
by red sugar water,
nasturtium, cosmos,
purple coneflower.

How much longer
can each miracle
be made, when
with your absence

comes this pain—
bold as the leaves
in flame when
the first rain arrives?

Jaime Asaye FitzGerald

At the Hollywood Downtowner

It would seem impossible
to make love behind *fire-proof*
and sound-proof red brick,
where people fuck through mirrors
and the lobby smells like curry—

where a trickle of water
dribbles from the tap,
needles shoot from the showerhead,
and the towels, so dry,
leave my body sapped.

But no less likely behind
the glacial façades, the sheer cliffs
of accommodation up the street,
where love is rendered
with surgical precision.

Yet here where neon cackles
and the sheets prick,
I whisper, *I love you,* in his ear,

and in the broken-bottle morning
the wicked also cry,
Agggh, I luff you! I luff you!
while overhead, rock the beds.

SUNG YOL YI

The Cheap Motel

When I was too poor to rent a quiet room,
I couldn't sleep much.
Each night a sound like an animal's moan
Came through the walls from a woman's throat.

The young couple who rented the next room
Argued in the evening,
Made the sounds of love in the night,
And whispered all through the dawn.

At first my girlfriend protested, "Oh no!"
And stubbornly covered her face with a blanket.
But after hearing the moans from the next room,
She turned toward me and began to unbutton slowly
In a cheap motel.

Sung Yol Yi

The Belt

When I get up in the morning
And buckle up my belt,
I am ready.

Though it is only a strip of leather,
It changes our lives as the Serpent
Changed Adam. He went
To look for some clothes.
He put on his belt.
It protects us from shame or cold,
And makes us honorable to the world.

It energizes me like Samson's hair.
The necktie is attractive
But it could be dangerous
And makes us weak and timid
Like a salaried man facing the lay-off.

That hot summer in *Seoul*,
When meat was in high demand,
A thief butcher pounded
My dog, *Baduk*, for a stew.
He was wearing a collar not a belt.
The animals including my dog
Are dominated by human because they
Don't know how to tie the belt.

In the sixteenth century, my hero admiral Yi
Fought the Japanese for seven years
And lost not a battle. How?
He invented the turtle ship, used superior strategy
And first of all, for seven years, never unbuckled
His belt.

110

Sung Yol Yi

Soong-Nyung/ Rice Tea

It's the principle of total consumption:
A cooker emptied of its rice,
Still has a slightly burned layer on its bottom.
Just pour in drinking water and boil.

When I was young, after missing the day's meals,
During the barley time of *boree-gogae**
When we had to wait for the harvest,
That savory smell from the neighbor's
Drove me to hunger
Like the smell from a mother's breasts.

But lucky you.
You don't have to bother boiling burned rice.
Lately a Japanese company has produced
Rice tea in bags,
And the taste is not bad.

*A Korean Slang of barley harvest time

JUDITH TERZI

L.A. Retro-Specs

I fell for your rock & roll blitz. Buffed
bucks, skirts & sweaters matched. First

Revlon & Maybelline. Count the times
at Rexall's photo booth. You dig? Together

waiting for b & w squares to ooze out.
So fine. Onion rings, luv, if I hadn't had

them, I would have loved you ½ as much.
Ditto for pastrami at Canter's in the borscht

belt where I lived. Hail to prune Danish
& hair-netted waitresses whose jungle red

lipstick spilled way over lip limits. I fell
under your spell. Honest I did. And Dean's

& Newman's & Natalie's & Tab's & Sal's.
Kisses for the souls of the departed cool

whose autographed glossies I tacked
to my wallpaper roses. Amen. Amen. Just

you & me slow dancing to Mathis & Cooke
& Cole. Remember Brando in his red

Triumph next to my two-tone green Chevy
Bel Air? Both of us on a Sunset Boulevard

curve headed for the sea. Then alone with
Heston in an elevator during my first quake.

Thou shalt not panic, Charlton preached.
How I reveled in your Saturdays—safe

as parents imagined them—riding the bus
to Grauman's Chinese or the Egyptian or

Judith Terzi

Wallach's Music City, Sunset & Vine, where
I listened to 78s then 45s in soundproof booths.

Undiscoverable & pure, I was no starlet, baby,
just an ordinary girl pedal-pushing through

a shake-rattle-and-roll-about-to-explode decade.

Openings

Workshopping a poem in the Inland
Empire. On the sleeve of my latte:
John: 4:4-26. A Google search finds
Jesus parched at Jacob's Well. He asks
a Samaritan woman for water. My rug

whirls in a womb of Mrs. Meyers
at Sierra Bonita Launderette. A woman
folding sheets asks me for gum and
opinion. *Would it be okay if I didn't go
to my mother's funeral*? A dozen other

people, yet I am chosen. The Samaritan
woman wonders why a Jew would ask
her for water. Black cloth shrouds
the woman behind me at a Target
checkstand. I flinch. She is wearing

a niqab, covered from head to toe
with only a slit for her eyes. I wish
I hadn't flinched. The woman folding
sheets says she got faith from her *suegra*—
her mother-in-law; her mother gave

Judith Terzi

abuse. We unveil feelings at Classic
Coffee in the Inland Empire. This could
be a breakthrough poem. Missionaries
in Israel convert Jewish orphans. I was
the only Jew at Clinton Elementary. Every

other child left for catechism twice a week.
Silent, embarrassed, I memorized Wordsworth
and the Hebrew alphabet. Why do we still
lean close each time we whisper *Jewish*?
From our sidewalk table, we hear barking,

train whistles, motorcycles. Jesus tells
the Samaritan woman *salvation comes
only through the Jews.* Here, we worship
revelation. The launderette woman says
her mother was always beat up. *Press*

charges? How could she? It was the devil,
she answers. I stare into the eyes of the Target
woman. Pools of perception, luminous blue
like my mother's. *I love your beret*, she says.
My rug is barely visible, only an occasional

fault line appearing: hegemony of foam. I lay
my days-of-the-week panties on the counter
at Target checkstand #10. *A different pastel
for each day*, says the covered woman
in pure American. New Testaments lie open

on every other table at Classic Coffee. My
parents closed windows when they argued.
Closed Venetian blinds when we lit
the menorah. I never invited anyone over
in December: no Christmas tree. We hear

someone say he found Jesus on the soccer
field in junior high. Sartre's Garcin says:
Hell is other people. L'enfer, c'est les autres.
If such is the case, there can be no poem.
Fresh chosen morning brew. Mini cinnamon

Judith Terzi

rolls. Foam skims the hills until noon
pollution. Fire season in Southern California.
No rain in Jerusalem either. The woman
folding sheets says her brother fondled her
daughters. She has mastered the zen of

fitted-sheet folding: None of her sheets
become cotton percale amoebas like mine.
She has altars in her home: candles burning
for the *Señora del Perpetuo Socorro* or
the *Virgen de Juquila*, Señora of Oaxaca.

Motorized angels lounge in ceramic
fountains. My machine stops. *This facility
is under twenty-four hour video surveillance*:
My oversudsing has become recorded
Sierra Bonita Launderette history. I pay

for the days-of-the-week pastel panties
at checkstand #10, lurk behind a ringing
Salvation Army bell. The covered woman
drives off in a silver Hyundai Sonata.
Breakthrough keeps pooling inside the poem

PATTY SEYBURN

What I Disliked about the Pleistocene Era

The pastries were awfully dry.
An absence of hummingbirds—
of any humming, and birds' lead
feathers made it difficult to fly.

Clouds had not yet learned
to clot, billow, represent.
Stars unshot, anonymous.
Moon and sun indifferent.

No one owned a house, a pond,
a rock on which to rest your head.
No arc, no here then there. Beginning
meant alive. The end was dead.

Art still a ways away—no lyre.
Beauty, an accident. Needs
and wants bundled like twigs
then set on fire. Except, no fire.

Candles had no wicks. Fruit
lacked seed. Books bereft of plot.
Ornament and condiment
were empty cisterns. There *were* pots.

It was pure act. No motivation,
consequence, imagination.
Sometimes, a flare, a glow, a gleam.
No questions asked. No revelation.

And I was not yet capital I.
Still just an eye. No mouth,
no verb, no AM to carry dark
from day, dirt or sea from sky—

God not God until one dove
called out, "where the hell's dry land?"
An answer formed. A raven shrugged
and toed a line across the sand.

New, the sand. New, the vast
notion of this long division.
New, the understanding that
this time, there would be no revision.

November

In heaven, there are two
of everything, in case
one breaks. Always a back-
up plan: two Zambonis
for the firmamental
ice rink, because the dead
like to glide around a lot,
cutting cunning figures
of sideways eight. Two large
needles with generous
eyes and two spools of thick
navy thread to stitch the
wayward stars into their
god-named constellations –
they fall from formation,
sometimes, on the nights you
hear amateurs complain,
I can't find the Big Dipper
or the two bright lights of
Queen Cassiopeia
or explaining to loved
ones that it's too damn dark,
when the truth is, some rogue
star is loose up there
and archangels are poor
seamstresses which leaves the
task to us—flaw, husk, raw
edge—and once dead it is
not easy to fix things.

Patty Seyburn

Long Distance

My mother calls me for the first time from the afterlife.
I am pleased to hear her voice, her tough-broad, film noir syntax,
        her old-world dubious tone.
It's not so great here, she says.
She must have run into my Aunt Toots.

The Talmud says, *Better one hour there than a lifetime here* and
        better one hour here than a lifetime there.
I hope the Angel of Death knows: you cannot silence my mother.
Steal her breath, still her tongue, sew shut her lips, export her soul –
        it's no use.
The pencil-chewing, beehived operators of the cosmos will always
        put through her calls.

When she calls again, I will tell her how beautifully the cantor sang
        at her funeral, how much we praised her, how many
        people attended.
It was a cast of millions.
There were a dozen limos.
She will know I am lying.
She raised me to be a bad liar.

We prefer doing things we're good at.
I am a fine dweller on subjects that sadden me.
The whistles and bells of remorse and mortality
        are my stock-in-trade.
I am a serviceable alto, though I should never be given a solo.
The Talmud says, *It would be nice if you had a point.*

This is my problem, of late: all lines, some planes, no points.
I am expansive and linear, but cannot reach a conclusion.
I tell my mother, *the world is full today.*
A hummingbird hovers near my voice.
I wonder if it will fly in and release my vocal chords
        from the burden of service.
What would I do, could I not speak?

Patty Seyburn

I was raised to sit eighth-row center and comb the clearance rack,
       to fear the law and eat canned peas, to excel.
It served me well, give or take.
My mother asks, *do you have any coins in your pocketbook?*
When I was young, she forbade long distance calls.
They were for rich people.
The middle class spoke locally.

Ma, don't go.
I rummage around in my pockets, wallets and change-purse, plunge
       my hands into the couch's seams.
No luck in Mudville.
My mother hums, "Mean to Me" with a little vibrato.
My mother says, *they want me to get on a bus.*

HÉLÈNE CARDONA

Notes From Last Night
—to John, in memory of his father

One can distinguish Van Gogh from Chagall,
that state of in-betweenness
where even objects seem alive—
to do with light and looking pure.
Because of all this light, I'm partially blind.
It doesn't matter whose ghost you see
as long as you see one.
Two darknesses together across the shape
of face, warmth comes forward, cool retreats.
I just experience.
Talk about faith I don't believe,
experience is cellular.
In our normal state we're not able to perceive,
that's why I think the dead know.
I had never before seen the beauty
of it, everything has to do with light.
Every ghost proof of the afterlife,
any ghost.

STEPHEN YENSER

Paradise Cove

My daughter in the coastal sunset asks for Plato. "Plato,"
She begs, "blue Plato, please, Plato" . . .   Finally, I understand

And rummage from the picnic basket the Play-Doh, the blue can,
And the pink as well—which henceforth I call "Aristotle."

"Ariso'l, Ariso'l," she repeats—then, swallowing the glottal,
"Aerosol," and there we are, playing with both ideas that there are.

For one, this mixogamous world is all one thing, and for the other,
This waxing unicity is always two (or more, which is the same,

Since to rub two things together in a ruttish realm is to get others,
And those yet others, viz. our daughters and their sons).

The temporizing third idea—that these two are somehow one—
Returns us to the first. So Marcus Aurelius thought. Maybe Lao Tzu.

In any event, Nietzsche teaches that each thinker's goal and due
Is to become as serious as a child at play, even as the sun sinks,

Even when again the sun is setting—or rather, here in Los Angeles,
City of Angles, the set is sunning—stunning,

Even, in ever acuter, gentler rays that with the smaze
Turn the horizon Technicolor pinks and blues, lavenders and zincs.

CANDACE PEARSON

The Neurologist

How old are you? he asks from behind the plane
of his broad oak desk.

>Two hundred eighty eight, my mother answers.

He scribbles on his pad of paper. What do you call
this object I'm holding?

>An object, she says. (It's a number 2 pencil, but
>I'm not allowed to give hints.)

Yes, yes, its name?

>Name it whatever you'd like.

Who is President of the United States?

>My mother laughs in a way that mimics the sharp light
>sliced by the venetian blinds.
>Well, it used to be George Washington.

Who is the *current* President?

>If it matters so much to you, I'm sure we could
>look it up.

Tell me, what is 2 times 6?

>A problem.

As we leave,
he pats me on the shoulder, whispers,
You've got your hands full there.

>That was a bad man, she says when we reach
>the sidewalk. All the way home, at each red light,
>she slaps her hands against the dashboard—*Go. Go. Go.*

122

Candace Pearson

My Brother is Busy

My brother is busy packing for jail. I sit on his bed and watch him
set aside a blank notebook, pen, copy of Genet's "Thief's Journal."
Jean Genet did some of his best writing in prison, he tells me.

I want to say, he was a glamorous playwright in Paris, France,
you are a drug addict-sometime singer in Bakersfield, California.
Jean-Paul Sartre will not be coming to your rescue. Instead,

I say, *I'm not sure they'll let you have that fountain pen.*
The romance of jail, of positive spins, has captured my brother
in the June-addled San Joaquin Valley. He's hoping that this time

the judge will sentence him to a prison rehab unit. I'm done caring
what he hopes, or so I think, only here to pick up what's left of mine
that he hasn't pawned, then return to school. My first summer

on parole from stomach pumpings, bail bondsmen, high dramas
in the house on Occidental Street. *I can write with anything.* He removes
the pen from the stack. *I can write in dust, I can write with my mind.*

Here is the part where the sister laughs, where she may later wish
for a chance at revision. We don't know it, but this is our last
        conversation.
My brother will be dead in two weeks, I'll be in some other city

when he overdoses on downers as our parents drink double
vodka tonics in another room. I'll get a call at 2 am. Someone
will say, *This is your mama speaking.* And I'll answer, *Who?*

123

CECE PERI

It's Noir

For some people it's hard knowing what's noir and what's not.
−Max Bloom

—for Max Bloom, who knows

If there's a hitchhiker
  border crossing
    or sudden change of plans
if someone's named Vera
  The Wall
    or Lola Molina
if there's a knife fight
  gun fight
    or bare knuckle justice
if a guy
  lights a match
    with his thumb
if someone's after payback
  a payroll
    or the lay of a lifetime
if the dead
  are buying land
    out in the valley
if there's a car
  a cliff
    and a claims adjuster
if a wife buys a black veil
  before she needs
    a black veil
if it's night
  if it's raining
    if the music's complicit
the drugs are illicit
  the whole set up–
    suspicious
if the guy you're rooting for
  winds up hugging
    a manhole cover
if even
  the moon

124

Cece Peri

ends up in the gutter
and if nobody ever
   had a chance
     to begin with
                  it's noir.

Trouble Down the Road

At the flat top grill, he was all business,
flung raw eggs dead center into the corned beef
hash like a strapping southpaw.

In the alley, with me, he was all ideas.
Said he'd be leaving soon, had a shot back east—
a tryout for the big leagues.

Said his sister would loan him a Buick convertible,
and he'd fill it with malt beer and tuna.
All he needed was a woman to hold

his cat while he drove.
I like animals, I told him. Then I dropped
my cigarette into the dusty clay,

ground it out, slow,
felt the road under my foot.

Cece Peri

The White Chicken Gives a First-Hand Account
—from an Associated Press story

I love the red
wheelbarrow
rusting
by the barn,
my sturdy
nesting place,
my refuge
the night
raccoons
laid waste
the coop,
killed all
the laying hens
but me.

Farmer
buried them
in the far yard,
and Laslo,
the brown dog,
dug them
back up,
nuzzled each
gray bundle
against the long
hen house
and, there,
all morning
stood guard.

Laslo,
brother of my heart.

MARILYN ROBERTSON

One of Nine Dogs Taking Obedience Training at Griffith Park

We're out early,
a motley pack in shades
of brown, medium sized—
cockers, terriers, mixes—
yet we move as one,
our collars tight, all nine
leashes in his hand.

He's collected us,
one by one,
from our apartments.
Our people
have abandoned us
to him.

If we slow or turn
our heads, he hisses.
On the park's dirt path,
we trot, stop, sit, stay.

He drops all nine
leashes, struts a ring
around us. We think,
we could run away,
but we don't move.

Other dogs rush by
with their people who
pull them as they jog,
talk and eat.

Our noses quiver
but we hold them high.
Our attention is focused,
our ears perked.

Marilyn Robertson

When he says trot,
we trot. He stops, we stop.
His finger points, we sit;
we lie down; we stay.

We're not sure why.
We don't even know who he is.

How to Eat a California Orange
for Curt

A rancher's son, he knows about oranges.
I watch the way his practiced hands surround it,
measure its size and weight,

the way he probes below the navel,
takes his time, presses in on sun-blushed
skin with thumbs,

spirals down and around as if sculpting something
out of clay. He loosens its resistance, pulls back
the stringy pith, the skin a shell

that he rejoins as if intact, the fruit
fully exposed. He spreads apart the sections—
the air grows tart. He hands me one,

takes another up to meet his lips.
When they're ripe, he tells me, they come
off the tree right in your hand.

LUCIA GALLOWAY

One Harvest
—August, 1962, California

Where irrigation water seeps
all summer   into sandy soil   I balanced
on   a   truck bed
to the peach orchard   unloaded
with   my   bare   hands
rough   splintery   planks   and set them
to support   branches heavy   with fruit.
This is how the marriage started.   And
home   at 5:00   from   a day
at the conveyor-belt—my shift
grabbing   peaches   out   of   moving
boxes   sorting them
by size   into   a grid of crates—
I picked up   then   a knife
for that   late   hour
halving   more   fruit   separating   the halves
from   their   seeds   laying them
in rows   on drying trays
for the sulfur shed.
We had   no garlic then   except
what passed us   on the road   to   Gilroy.

ERIKA AYÓN

Apá's Eden

As dawn breaks through the crimson curtains,
you rise, kiss Amá goodbye, the only time
I see you do this, drive away,
circles of dust and tire marks remain.

You return four months later with the trunk full
of crates of strawberries, peaches, apricots,
grapes, plums. The nectar seduces our lips,
seeps through our fingers. Our nights fill
with dreams of this Garden hidden
in the center of the valley.

Most nights you sit in the dark, speak
of how the strawberries bleed onto your cut,
blistered hands. How people are plucked
from trees by the immigration police.

You whisper about a scornful sun, of being
forced by a landowner to hold a blue whistle
between your lips so you won't be tempted
to consume the fruits you pick. The sound
of whistles fused with the rustle of the wind
fills the field like a song.

Erika Ayón

Love Letter to Octavio

Octavio Paz, I did the unspeakable,
I tore a poem from one of your poetry books
at the library. It was an impulse thing,
my library card was in my wallet.
I did not care that there were witnesses;
the man with the gold framed glasses
in the next aisle, the librarian with the curly bob.
I read the poem and felt you were speaking
to me. I was the *niña* in the poem who cried,
who prayed, whose skies turned into battlefields.
I tore it as a desire to have you, to take you
with me. I had never fallen in love with a poem,
with a poet, like I fell in love with you that day.
If you must know, I still have the ripped poem.
I keep it in a secret place as if it were a love letter.

The year was 1998, I was sixteen,
attending high school in El Sereno,
you were in Mexico, dying of cancer.
I imagined you overlooking the landscape
of Mexico, the way the mountains murmured
in the distance, you sipping dark coffee,
your wife Marie-José behind you,
her arms holding you like a *rebozo*.
Poems circle above your head like crows.

Years later, I sent a copy of the book to the library,
the library that had been my safe haven
in my teens, no return address, just a blue post-it
with the word "Donation," all the pages intact.
By that time, I had learned to let go of poetry,
I no longer felt like a young girl,
I was a woman writing my own poems down,
before the wind blew them away.

Erika Ayón

Thirteenth Child

I am my father's thirteenth child.
I confess this to my friend Mehnaz
over an iced Moroccan Tea at Coffee Bean.
Mehnaz who majored in Religion and Numbers
lights up, "Thirteen is a lucky number,
that's the number of my parking space
at Moorpark High School."

All my life I have felt unlucky.
Feeling unlucky, I have gone to a *curandera*
on Lankershim Blvd. to get a *limpia.*
In my indigo blue bathing suit,
the *curandera's* instructions—
I bent over to kiss the feet of saints,
sprinkled holy water on my skin,
recited prayers for protection.

One October full moon,
I stood outside my apartment building on Irolo,
whispered wishes into a bottle of water,
swung the water over my left shoulder.
Esmeralda, the fortune teller had told me
to do this after she read my cards,
she saw my unlucky life.

If I had given the palm reader
with the big plasma T.V. in his living room,
more money when he asked, he would have
told me which dark haired man to avoid.
The lines of my palms revealed to him
my sad life, his brown eyes uncovered
in my palm a shallow pool, not an endless
river of possibilities.

I want to tell Mehnaz
that when she pulls into her parking space,
when she steps out of her car,
to think of me, to recite a prayer,
dance ritualistically, dust her feet,
she who studied Gods.

132

SARAH MACLAY

—as, after Odysseus, her body wanted to be Ophelia

The pistol came with its own music.
An echo slid from her throat:
Liquid, alive beyond common names for color.
How at night she could not swim.
Her song like a line of neon in wavering slices
across the crinoline dark
until the dogs began to bay
and men slipped into the skins of animals
to roll against the mud without the barrier of clothes.
How that bay was a living jewel—the sound, the topaz water—
the water had poured from her
and become alive.
She would wash up on the shore or float,
as white as the lizard who pulls the carriage
in a dream, all soggy finery
and hair and reeds.
Over and over
her body was painted
in darkness,
like a wine of skin.
What was true:
It was up to her to invent
her own music,
as she began to hear it
in the growing stain of sky.

Sarah Maclay

Grille

As if through glass, through windows, in a café, in the afternoon or early
evening, in June, in June or November, month like a fetish of gray—a
month of water hanging onto itself; until it drizzles, a month of dulled
light—he is seen for a moment, accidentally, between appointments, in
the middle of errands, walking down steps, the cement steps, say, of an
old bank—old enough for granite, for columns—pulling his keys out of
his pocket, or gripping the small black remote that replaces keys (which
you can't hear the sound of, behind all this glass), and approaching his
car, so that for an instant you see his face unguarded—or as unguarded
as you will see it—and you try to memorize it, but it's too fleeting, so
that now only the back of his head, and maybe the veins in his arms that
you memorized before (the way his fingers go, his shirt)—or the waiter
comes, the waiter comes by and asks if you've decided, the waiter
comes by and asks if you've made up your mind—

but this is the opposite of confession.

ELENA KARINA BYRNE

Of Him, This Vertigo: Breath Mask

*If a man breathed a woman's vapor, his breath soul would be weakened
and his mind would become fuzzy and lose its power to focus on the hunt.*
-The Living Tradition of Yup'ik Masks,
Ann Feinup-Riordan

Now her breath.
Now the whole air from her mouth pushed inside his, exhaled hours later
into his hands before going to bed. Now her breath like dropped
pebbles' rings, moving, slow into their own transparency, left on his
   pillow
as the already unfolding half-wing of the face,
dream-inhale and sexual double notes. Now the mind is good measure
and what you can't see won't hurt you. Now he's still weak at the edge
of her body and her breathing. Now halfway strange to himself, halfway
apparitional. Now dizzy, he is the undermusic of her speech, all the way
down darkness. Now the uncut white paper wind.
Now the past who inherits them both. Now the distance between sky
and falling, inner ear aria. Now and now, being alive like that,
never contained in vanishing and reoccurring. Now aspiration,
   expectation.
Now the century's stronghold, lucent circle above their heads.
Now the nothing made of them making sound.
Now nothing he can do. Now the cliff.
Now her breath.

Elena Karina Byrne

Moon Mask

The moon's best lover,—
                                    -Hart Crane

White domain.
Black domain.

     Bleached flour and salt of him,
his head hung with paper orchids and goat bells
over the black water, heavy
from the balcony.
Not this King, great
burlap octopus who came out
to see his subjects, the chipped riff-raff
of stars and ignited gas, this scalawag, he
whose reign is loss and umbilical gut-
wrenching desire, no, not him,
whose open-boat skeleton slowly drifts
through the Queen's gate, a great white
glare, unpolished in its welter of stolen light
to the heart's content from a fisticuffs of distance,
or Varuna with orders for the seasons
riding sea monster by night
to take on the brood elegy of the past
one domino at a time, no, no, not the monarchy
when the sky was always there, dogma-
dark, not that, not him, but
behind the rule of waves, slipped from
his silver Orphean lock, another face,
tossed coin, a new time
just for you and your pound of flesh,
the sweet exchange made for his mouth
when he comes to you, stripped
of sadness and once royal blood, to bear
his white chest, his unclenched figure of speech
and hold court, making his steep climb
from the unfinished wood chair
to the sky on this *monan dag*, day of the moon,
night of the moon, rising
in his heat, as far as you will know, into
the arms of the perfect you,

perfect stranger.

136

LOIS P. JONES

Kensington Concierge

At 3:00 a.m. I am wide open as the window
with only a small offering from the moon.
Night brings London's ghosts – stray thoughts

of streetwalkers climb the flues,
and take root. This room holds its hurts –
swollen feet, bent neck, the width of the lift

when you looked at me this evening.
Some part of us rose to the surface
then silvered as it sank. An odd pull,

like a thread in the underwing, but I kept
from touching your velvet yarmulke,
rubbed my voice for a path to speak.

I know you. You are dark oil
in a new lamp and even if you give
your hours to the opening of doors,

or the recovery of what's lost –
the red glove or gentleman's cufflink,
my leather diary full of words of you

forgotten on the clean sheets, you are still
my keeper of the lantern, aglow in your raven suit,
its black cotton so close to my fingers.

I've only had one tryst in my life,
but Levi I would break the rule for you –
break it like matzo on a candled night. I want

to hear you explain the strange razor calls
of rooftop birds. Our vowels rain-lipped –
the husky sounds of quiet need. You are

the kind of man who looks with your whole body.
Come here in your night coat like a Cossack.
Come in – your dark curls still, untouched.

LUIS J. RODRIGUEZ

Palmas

Palmas swayed on a rickety porch
near an old eaten-up tree
and plucked at a six-string:
The guitar man of the 'hood.

Fluid fingers moved across the neck
like a warm wind across one's brow.

Each chord filled with pain,
glory and boozed-up nights.

Every note sweating.

On Saturdays, Palmas jammed with local dudes.
They played in his honor on the nights
he didn't show up.

The guitar man—so sick, so tired,
but, man, he played so sweet.

I often wondered what gave Palmas his magic.
Blues bands wanted him.
Norteño bands wanted him.
Jazz musicians called out his name
from the bandstand.

He played Wes Montgomery
as if the dude were living inside his head.

He played crisp *corridos* and *Jarocho* blues
and seemed to make Jeff Beck
float through the living room window.

Yet he didn't venture too far beyond his rickety porch.
Sometimes he sat alone in his room,
the guitar on a corner of an unmade bed.

The last I heard, he played only
when the heroin in his body
gave him a booking.

Luis J. Rodriquez

The Monster

It erupted into our lives:
two guys in jeans shoved it through the door
—heaving & grunting & biting lower lips.

A large industrial sewing machine.
We called it "the monster."

It came on a winter's day,
rented out of mother's pay.
Once in the living room
the walls seemed to cave in around it.

Black footsteps to our door
brought heaps of cloth for mama to sew.
Noises of war burst out of the living room.
Rafters rattled. Floors farted
—the radio going into static
each time the needle ripped into fabric.

Many nights I'd get up from bed,
wander squinty-eyed down a hallway
and peer through a dust-covered blanket
to where mama and the monster
did nightly battle.

I could see mama through the yellow haze
of a single light bulb.
She slouched over the machine.
Her eyes almost closed.
Her hair in disheveled braids,

each stitch binding her life
to scraps of cloth.

CHARLES HARPER WEBB

Marilyn's Machine

She bought it because her baseball player didn't want her to,
because her playwright and her President and her Attorney
General disapproved. *You're a star,* they said: the one
thing they agreed on. *Stars don't wash their own clothes.*

Too timid to defy them, she rented a little room
and brought her purchase there, safe in its cardboard box.
Disguised in a black wig and flowered muumuu,
she sat and stared at the machine, imagining the famous

bras, nylons and panties, tight sweaters and skirts
sighing as they rocked, settling down into the warm
detergent bath. Sometimes she cried, thinking
of the men who dreamed about her clothes and what

went in them. How many orgasms had she inspired,
who'd never had one of her own, her breathy voice
warding off "Was it good for you?" She loved
selecting temperatures: hot/warm, warm/cold, cold/cold,

and her favorite, hot/cold. She loved the brand name
"Whirlpool Legend." She loved the cycles,
especially "Rinse" and "Spin." She whispered their names,
thinking of a man thinking of her some distant day

when she is nothing but an image made from movies,
photos, gossip, exposés—an image thinking of him
thinking of her in her black wig and flowered muumuu,
rinsing, spinning till the dirt is washed away.

Charles Harper Webb

Wedding Dress

She wants it and she doesn't want it: the lace neck
and sleeves, the waist so tight she'll need it re-fitted
the day before *the* day. She wants and doesn't want
the pleats and puffs and bows, the veil's force field
guarding her face, the train's long barge dragging behind,
the whole creation so elaborate she must be lowered
into it—like a knight onto his horse—with a crane.

She wants and doesn't want to choose her neckline:
bertha, bateau, jewel, Queen Anne, décolletage;
her sleeves: *bishop, balloon, pouf, gauntlet, mutton leg;*
her silhouette: *ballgown, basque, empire, sheath, mermaid;*
her headpiece: *pillbox, derby, wreath, tiara, garden hat.*
She wants and doesn't want the four-page guest list,
the country club that overlooks the valley

like a war party, eager to attack. She wants
and doesn't want the triptych invitations,
the florist/psychic who intones, "I envision one black
vase per table, each holding a single white rose."
"I love him," she thinks, "but my Zeppelin tapes are melting;
my Bowie posters curling into flame. I love him,
but Uni High is vanishing like our senior *Brigadoon.*

I love him but my friends are turning into toasters,
china place settings, crystal salad bowls."
She wants and doesn't want the plane door closing,
Tahiti rushing toward her, then dropping behind,
Mom in her fuchsia gown starting to stoop,
Dad giving her away as white hair falls: a fairy ring
around his feet. Even as she pays for it, her dress

is yellowing, the wedding pictures aging into artifacts,
her children staring at strangers: one in a penguin suit,
one in her glory. They can't believe that living

Charles Harper Webb

works this way—just as the boy can't believe what else
his pecker will be for; the girl, where babies grow,
how they get there, what every month will leak from her.
"I want it, but I don't want it," she'll say.

Tenderness in Men

It's like plum custard at the heart of a steel girder,
cool malted milk in a hot bowling ball.

It's glimpsed sometimes when a man pats a puppy.
If his wife moves softly, it may flutter like a hermit thrush

into the bedroom, and pipe its pure, warbling tune.
Comment, though, and it's a moray jerking back into its cave.

Dad taught me to hide tenderness like my "tallywhacker"—
not to want or accept it from other men. All I can do

for a friend in agony is turn my eyes and, pretending
to clap him on the back, brace up his carapace with mine.

So, when you lean across the table and extend your hand,
your brown eyes wanting only good for me, it's no wonder

my own eyes glow and swell too big for their sockets
as, in my brain, dry gulleys start to flow.

Charles Harper Webb

Parasites

I was pumping my red Huffy—we couldn't afford Schwinn—
through the woods with Davey Kingman, my best friend.

> His ten-speed came from England, via his weird dad,
> whose greenhouse full of orchids ate up their back yard:

pink, white, yellow, purple, blood-red *parasites,*
Davey called them, since they leeched life out of wood.

> Locusts rattled as we rode. (It was June, I think.)
> Forbidden thoughts sucked at my brain like black orchids

sprung from the stump when, last Christmas, my folks
chopped down Santa. Like him, God knew everything,

> supposedly; yet when I palmed a quarter from the church
> collection plate, bought baseball cards, and scored

two Mickey Mantles, He didn't punish me. Nothing bad
happened when Dad cursed, "Jesus Christ!"—unless

> Mom heard. No God paralyzed Mick Jagger's hips
> or stopped The Stones grinding on Davey's transistor radio

as we rattled to our "fort" behind the Double Tree,
its locusts loud as fighter jets. (Or was it Mom's shock,

> gathering? Or God's world-wrecking rage?)
> Why was it good to believe water-to-wine and rising-

from-the-dead, but stupid to believe Donnie Atzenhofer,
who swore on the Bible, "My pa-paw struck out Babe Ruth"?
> In two years, these woods would be gone. Houses
> would spring from the dead roots, full of new kids

playing host to the old lies. The whole world hung—
a slide in a projector—poised to change as I spit out,

like a tapeworm, "I don't believe in God."
Davey's face went dark under the Double Tree.

"Me neither," he said finally, then tore away, me close
behind, soaring like the Apollo space ship, free of gravity

while, loud as booster-engines, sap-sucking locusts
roared.

JERRY GARCIA

How to Bury Your Dad
To my daughters

Find yourself a yellow '67 Volkswagen
with overheating pistons;
call it your "V dub ya bug."
It will burn plenty of fluid.

Careful not to double-clutch
that steep, winding grade
from Santa Rosa to Trinidad.
Enter the fabled shading
of ocean trees
where scents of decomposing air,
old foliage and a bear's
organic spray saturate
the Redwood bark.

Don't fret traveling-day doldrums.
When you tire of driving,
pull off to the side of the road,
let the Humboldt runoff
mottle your boots.
Eat coarse salami, crusty bread
and cheddar cheese.
Your front trunk should carry laundry,
oranges and a red & blue cooler
full of Budweiser and Perrier.

If the fuel line chokes
find a traveling neighbor
to push downhill
until torque overcomes stall.

Soon you'll get to a downgrade clearing
with glimpses of Pacific Ocean
through burley Redwood Goliaths.
Seek a wooded rise
where clouds and mountain peaks are level,
stop and smoke a reefer among the ferns.

Jerry Garcia

When the road levels,
dust my ashes, your geezer dad,
into pine needles and sod;
litter the Avenue of Giants
with my remains.

Rest.

Then carry on to Meyer's Flat, Scotia, Rio Dell,
those peculiar forest towns leading toward Eureka bay.

Experience oil fogged air, northern kelp
and beach salt.
Take a sight seers' dalliance,
travel for days,
watch whales grace the depths
and pelicans claiming bays.

Be sisters, be friends.

Ride that rainy northerly jaunt
through haze and drizzle
'til your wipers fail.

LUÍS CAMPOS

At the Hospital

-Are you a relative?
She's in room 412,
Mental Health Clinic –
the attendant will unlock
the elevator door.

-Do not discuss unpleasant subjects,
do not ask difficult questions,
visit ends at nine;
if she cries, comfort and reassure her,
let her know that she's loved –
do not use words such as suicide
or income tax.

-Do not keep looking at your watch,
it may be necessary to repeat
what you say,
it may be necessary to repeat
what you say…

-If the patient is depressed,
do not attempt stand-up comedy,
maintain a hopeful attitude,
but don't cite examples
of insane people that have recovered.

-Do not use the word "nut" for any reason.
Should violence occur,
hum the secret word,
which today is "mantra."

-Enjoy your visit
and drink as much water as you wish.

Luís Campos

A North Hollywood Ending

—For Dave Dutton. Thank you.

-Went by the emptied
Dutton's Books on Laurel Canyon
& was surprised to see
Bukowski, Spillane, Capote & Wilde
on the sidewalk in front…
looking sad and somewhat bewildered.

-Was that a tear on Charles?
of course not! don't be silly!
and just because Mickey
was wiping his nose
didn't mean…

-The picture of Oscar Wilde
was one of gloom…
Truman looked devastated.

-The sadness was too heavy;
I turned to go,
and then I saw them…
thousands of men & women of letters,
led by Shakespeare,
Cervantes and Mark Twain,
followed by Dorothy Parker,
e.e. cummings, James Baldwin,
the Brontë sisters, Juan Ramón Jiménez…

-They marched in front
in silent protest,
then they were gone.

-The building remains.

HOLLY PRADO

Camus' 100th Birthday

a drug lord's newspaper photo: he's handsome.
above his tight mouth, that gorgeously-trimmed mustache.
and on the bus, a drunk next to my husband shouts at a stranger,
"you'll be a movie star by age twenty-five!"

beauty — sorry Keats — isn't always truth. yet, I believe
fragmentary brilliance: the moon tonight. she's scimitar,
sharpened glamour of illegality: an arrogance of beauty.

yes, that's our autumn now,
stolen goods. every friend's face ready to be arrested, to be
swept into fame, to be cut down before telling us what it all
means. a season partially paid for, the moon-boat loaded, ready

to get us high, to explode us, to — what?

to compel our impulsive bicycle rides across the freeway
when we can't stop, can't resist, can only love new ghosts:

the loyal friend
dead in the next month or two.

beauty: goodbye. old drunk: go home.

Holly Prado

Earning a Living

figs a lot of them stacked in plastic containers at Trader Joe's
and cheap   why resist when for $2.99 all that squish
that strange purple-black with pink at the stem
can be mine to bite   not a vampire bite   not a rabid
dog bite   but the healthy loving bite into fruit which
seems to actually enjoy its fate: being eaten
as we're all chomped on by whatever swallows us eventually.

figs luscious purple-black sexual pliable
nothing new can be said   we can only repeat
pliable   testicle   vaginal   the fig-eating scene
in "Women in Love" a movie which includes
two men wrestling   nude in front of a burning
fireplace   I have wanted a fig tree ever since Sarkis
elderly Armenian neighbor   planted his tree   I saw
how fast it grew   how abundant confident joyful

figs hung   on their huge-leaved branches
the lesson of age is this: often, more is denied
than granted so the guy at the nursery   someone

I sort of know because he's been there for years,
knowledgeable   sarcastic   only helpful if prodded
says there are no dwarf fig trees I could plant in a pot no
never   nothing like that   plant green beans instead.

I only have pots   many days, I only have the past,
that carefully-sharpened knife lodged in my shoulder
so that it hurts to dig up soil   a friend who's
the crunch of refusal against bone   I won't
cook with her again and will never myself have enough yard.

Sarkis said, "pick figs — go ahead, pick figs!"
Armenians are clanish but not selfish; my people   although
they planted this country with wheat and logic   didn't
teach me figness. So, I pick up the abundant figs at Trader Joe's
then set them where they ripen on my narrow countertop.
any redemption of the heart needs the body;
those men wrestle not to kill but to adore muscle as faith,
a painful shoulder as ready earth.

come, figs, grow here.

150

JAMES RAGAN

Rilke on the Conveyor Belt at Los Angeles International

A rick of pages, it falls hardly noticed
into motion, and down the track, unspined,
it cycles time between a rucksack and laundry.
A book no thicker than a wallet or a comb,
It is the unworthy carry-on, newly bought,
colliding with a carpetbag or steamer
on the unlikely navigation into being
where it's not. Each passenger has watched it
circle more than once, a bold intrusion
into the archipelago of things familiar.
There is no fixed point of concentration,
no laughter, no elation when the eyes dissect
the slow descent of baggage into orbit
as if in taking up an armstrap, each handler
slews a body to the spars of his shoulder.
Had Rilke, himself, fallen unbound,
lying in united state, he would have passed
unnoticed by the baggage check or porter
who fail to think it odd or such a pity
to tag him at the lost and found.
How many miles had his words trespassed,
how many cities, alive, unread
among so many ports of authority, a gold leaf
of art so grand in the pall of memory
it gives the mind encouragement to survive.
Unless unsung like a soldier's duffel, duty bound,
fear spreads its tarp along the spine of language.
Creation can end this way, abrupt and final,
like travel to the ends of the world
with no intent, or vision, but destination.

James Ragan

Shouldering the World

When I was tumbling young and hurried
and had no words to climb,
but knew the trees on the wide lawn
to shimmy and skin to scrape
into soft bleedings, I would bucket down
plums and black cherries for the scrolled batter
my mother kneaded with her thumbs,
each round pan a single flat globe
of busty dough above the juiced pickings,
and when, in season, Easter currants,
flowing sap along the walnuts I had crushed,
had laid their wintered wash of gravel
on the tongue in so many freshly spun orbits,
and given song to a mind deliciously green,
only then had I learned the world
was not with me as I thought it must,
and had I noticed more the play of metal,
rolling pin, spoon, and the shell cracker
or the miniature tin wheel that crimped and beveled
crust on the ledge of the pastry pan,
I would have known what hard earning
comes with pain for the work of the thing,
that the play of one force on another,
a roller flattening thin the skin of the matted flour
or the nut cracked quick into splits of progeny,
was the child's first true act of tending
each and every bruise the mind had buried
like a thought with the hard hammer of memory
on whose wide shoulder I carried
the terror of all the world's cruel anguish.

JENNY FACTOR

The Street Hawkers
for Robert Bowen

Who will speak for the fruit, abundant in the summer harvest?
This guy on the corner of San Gabriel & First, wearing

his red baseball cap backwards, salutes us
with a bag of silent cherries and leaps into traffic

with a jaunty hand.   Who will speak for crates of oranges
ripened on the tree, for the great waves of zucchini

trucking to the markets. And when the markets
turn them away, for the workers who take in

these fruity orphans and lift them up
on each summer corner

Like a flag, like a shield, like some dangling offer of surrender?
In median strips, beside shut Volvo windows,

along the routes of our endlessly going:
these orphans & these vegetables, these fruits & these orphans

In our country, in our America
with supplications and with foreign mouths

with winnowing eyes,   with calloused hands
every day ripening,   on every corner.

Who will speak for this abundance,
for this crop of summer that no one is buying?

Will you speak? Or you? Will I?

Jenny Factor

Malibu Noël

Christmas house of roasting rosemary, incense,
and the siren ocean whose song is sunset,
shaping wing and wave in the moment's treason:
daylight is falling.

Falling day, the sun with no sense of season
topples westward, splattering rose and ripple.
Eastward, lights respond to new night like dimmer
switches dragged upward.

In the low tide's clear-washed wet sand of evening,
doors swing wide, and families with their children
in red sweaters, lace, patent-leathers squeaking,
take to the beach. Their

German shepherds, Huskies flash teeth and wrangle,
nosing sand, they race through the posts of neighbors'.
Carpeting their fur in their play, they chase raw
seaweed like strangers.

From the tide-toed edges, a small boy bundles
with his shovel, waddling toward the wood stairs,
and his mother follows him with her scarf tied
against the wind chill.

There are those who make of such nights a goblet.
There are those who celebrate how the glimmer
of a live room closes up warm and sacred,
lives filled with children.

All my life, my strange eyes have seen the wrong things.
Missing one thing, settling on another.
Wiping up graffiti from sides of boulders,
clearing, erasing

Bald sunrise eclipsing the ashen woman
wandering on the sand with a mothy blanket.
Mimicking my mood, my perspective shifts off,
listless, mistaken.

154

"This is how I see," said Picasso pointing
to a canvas, Cubism's altered women,
"Sight's sequential, subject to subject feeling."
Eyes plucked like nipples.

So I'm looking west where the day's upended
like a toddler's punch, and the curlews argue
over fish. I keep to my back the shadows
milling around me.

Mirror of the pool shows our neighbor's perfect
pine extending ten feet and globed like bread fruit.
In the kitchen, seventy years is kneading
fresh loaves for dinner.

I can almost hear every wineglass set down
on the table, vibrating from its landing.
At the moment hands let an object settle,
everything's shaken.

Doors unlock, the families call their wandering
parties home and close up the house for nightfall.
Every staircase takes on its load of footsteps.
I watch the riptide.

Houses perch like nests on the seacliff. Houses,
camp fires on the bank of this primal endzone.
Shut inside, the season plays out its final
trumpet of yule time.

Christ but how the sky is a finished perfect
thought. Rose marred to amethyst in the knife fall.
What I do not choose to see in the margins
calls me to dinner.

TIMOTHY STEELE

Toward the Winter Solstice

Although the roof is just a story high,
It dizzies me a little to look down.
I lariat-twirl the cord of Christmas lights
And cast it to the weeping birch's crown;
A dowel into which I've screwed a hook
Enables me to reach, lift, drape, and twine
The cord among the boughs so that the bulbs
Will accent the tree's elegant design.

Friends, passing home from work or shopping, pause
And call up commendations or critiques.
I make adjustments. Though a potpourri
Of Muslims, Christians, Buddhists, Jews, and Sikhs,
We all are conscious of the time of year;
We all enjoy its colorful displays
And keep some festival that mitigates
The dwindling warmth and compass of the days.

Some say that L.A. doesn't suit the Yule,
But UPS vans now like magi make
Their present-laden rounds, while fallen leaves
Are gaily resurrected in their wake;
The desert lifts a full moon from the east
And issues a dry Santa Ana breeze,
And valets at chic restaurants will soon
Be tending flocks of cars and SUVs.

And as the neighborhoods sink into dusk
The fan palms scattered all across town stand
More calmly prominent, and this place seems
A vast oasis in the Holy Land.
This house might be a caravansary,
The tree a kind of cordial fountainhead
Of welcome, looped and decked with necklaces
And ceintures of green, yellow, blue, and red.

156

Timothy Steele

Some wonder if the star of Bethlehem
Occurred when Jupiter and Saturn crossed;
It's comforting to look up from this roof
And feel that, while all changes, nothing's lost,
To recollect that in antiquity
The winter solstice fell in Capricorn
And that, in the Orion Nebula,
From swirling gas, new stars are being born.

Haydn in Los Angeles

Surprise!—My off-ramp is closed!
As if to underscore
What's happening, the drum stroke
In Symphony 94
Bursts from the dashboard. Adding
Insult to irony
I'm late now, and "The Clock"
Comes next on this CD.

But that's the way with Haydn.
Uncannily, he frames
Conditions on our freeways
In his symphonies with names.
During "The Hornsignal"
I've been honked at from the rear,
And "The Miracle" played one morning
When the 405 was clear.

While speeders have blown by me,
I've listened to "The Chase."
(Perhaps "The Lamentation"
Solaced them when disgrace
And the CHP overtook them.)
Rightly or wrongly, I feel
"Il Distratto" applies to drivers
Texting at the wheel.

Timothy Steele

Too stormy and stressy for purists
And for romantics too prudent,
Mentor to Mozart and teacher
Of Beethoven (one tough student!),
Dear Haydn, your wife and patrons
Made you at times despair—
The former snipping your scores up
For paper to curl her hair.

Yet your symphonies still console us
And enlighten us as we drive—
One-hundred-and-four of them.
Or rather, one-hundred-and-five.
The last one's imaginary.
It features a plaintive flute
And a furious finale.
It's commonly called "The Commute."

158

RICK LUPERT

Homesick

It is on the fourth floor
of the Royal Ontario Museum
In Toronto, Ontario, Canada
that we see large photographs
of Los Angeles Freeways.
Thousands of miles from home
we cannot escape the traffic.

The Cheese King

We are impressed by the architecture
of the cheese at *La Fenice* on King Street.
The waiter tells us it is the King of Parmesan Cheese.

I ask if I should bow but
there is no time for my tomfoolery.
He tells us the story of the cheese.

In Italy as the second world war came
They would bury the cheese with
proper moisture to protect it from...

well he didn't say if they were protecting
it from the Nazis or the Allies.
I guess anyone would have wanted this cheese.

So they buried it as peasant cheese and then,
when the war was over, they dug it up and
it became King. This is the story of the cheese.

At another table they talk about how
Nancy Reagan has reunited with Ronny.
Across the street, something about Fellini.

I bow anyway. It's the least
I could do for the cheese
and the people who made it.

MIKE SONKSEN

The Arroyo Seco

Arts & Crafts flourished in the Arroyo Seco.
Chaparral hills with underground water flow,
most of the time, the dry creek's slow.

Homesteaders built craftsman homes
a century ago in Sycamore Grove.
Arts & Crafts flourished in the Arroyo Seco.

Poets & artists like Charles Fletcher Lummis
settled in the lush landscape of wooded oaks,
most of the time, the dry creek's slow.

The river ran wild a long time ago,
the concrete came for flood control;
Arts & Crafts flourished in the Arroyo Seco.

Figueroa is the intersection of the Avenues,
the river tunnels, the canvas for crews;
most of the time, the dry creek's slow.

Everything changed when the freeway was built,
concrete covered flowing water below;
Arts & Crafts flourished in the Arroyo Seco,
most of the time, the dry creek's slow.

DAVID ST. JOHN

Night

When Carole Laure stepped onto the black stage
At the Bobino, she got such a hand

That Lewis Furey, at the baby grand
Back in the shadows, had to grin. That image

Of her, singing in a single spotlight,
Hair rippling as she gave it a brief

Toss, just like in *Get Out Your Handkerchiefs*
Made us feel the world would be all right.

Later, drinking Armagnac at Le Dôme,
Watching the late-night Easter week parade

Down Montparnasse, I thought I saw, in a jade
& mauve raincoat, Carole Laure – walking home

With Lewis Furey, in a group of friends…
All laughing, as if the night would never end.

David St. John

VIII.

It was the night of tangerines. I mean, do you have ANY idea
What I'm talking about young Isadora-on-the-lam? Assembling, &
    dissembling.
Sliding back into the purple canvas world of the butterfly chair
By the floor-to-ceiling window looking out onto the pool, I watched
    the tiny
Auroras of the day break along the water into hieroglyphs of light,
Assembling ideograms of impermanence as you squeezed the bowl
    of tangerines
One by one against the glass cone ridges of the ancient juicer, the vodka
Beside you ice-flaked & fresh from the freezer, the parakeets in
    your daughter's
Room suddenly unlocking the sunset with their couplets, a little
    post-jungle
Hoodoo for the voodoo et cetera, & ohmigod that pink glass swizzle stick
With a hula dancer on top clinking in your glass. The savage blossoms
    rioting
In the garden, hibiscus hovering & mimosa starring the air, & of all
Of the taboos of the century, I had to fall in love with you. Later, the
    salamanders
Swarmed along the stream in your Japanese garden. Their leashes of
    silver ribbon
Still wet & dripping along the slick stones, & of all the bundles of
    frontiers
Still left for transgression, baby, I vote for this one & you.

David St. John

Gin

There's a mystery
By the river, in one of the cabins
Shuttered with planks, its lock
Twisted; a bunch of magazines flipped open,
A body. A blanket stuffed with leaves
Or lengths of rope, an empty gin bottle.
Put down your newspaper. Look out
Beyond the bluffs, a coal barge is passing,
Its deck nearly
Level with the water, where it comes back riding
High. You start talking about nothing,
Or that famous party, where you went dressed
As a river. They listen,
The man beside you touching his odd face
In the countertop, the woman stirring tonic
In your glass. Down the bar the talk's divorce,
The docks, the nets
Filling with branches and sour fish. Listen,
I knew a woman who'd poke a hole in an egg, suck
It clean and fill the shell with gin,
Then walk around all day disgusting people
Until she was so drunk
The globe of gin broke in her hand. She'd stay
Alone at night on the boat, come back
Looking for another egg. That appeals to you, rocking
For hours carving at a hollow stone. Or finding
A trail by accident, walking the bluff's
Face. You know, your friends complain. They say
You give up only the vaguest news, and give a bakery
As your phone. Even your stories
Have no point, just lots of detail: The room
Was long and bright, small and close, angering Gaston;
They turned away to embrace him; She wore
The color out of season,
She wore hardly anything at all; Nobody died; Saturday.
These disguises of omission. Like forgetting
To say obtuse when you talk about the sun, leaving
Off the buttons as you're sewing up the coat. So,
People take the little

David St. John

They know to make a marvelous stew;
Sometimes, it even resembles you. It's not so much
You cover your tracks, as that they bloom
In such false directions. This way friends who awaken
At night, beside you, awaken alone.

XIX.

"It was a day as *noir* as night." My own favorite line recently, rescued
From a notebook I've been tossing from jacket to suitcase to shoulder bag.
    Today
I am movement & simply all about movement & travel. In fact, I am
    moving
At this very moment on the *rapido* between Rome & Florence, & don't
    you
Find that in & of itself terribly, well, moving? I mean, the thought of me
Writing to you, writing this, moving here through this cinemagraphic
    journal
Of the soul, since that's how I think of this work, how it's lit by silence
& by pain — "the cinematography of the soul." Another not-so-bad line,
    eh? You
Tell me what makes this tolerable, you know, the pretention & arrogance
Of somebody announcing he's writing to you "on the *rapido* between
    Rome
& Florence," & in fact the only thing that makes it tolerable at all is
    knowing
This poem has nothing to do with Italy, nothing at all; though as you
    know, if
You know shit about me, or ever cared to, Italy is where my heart is
    (sappy, true,
& more exactly Rome is where my heart is; Florence, my mind &
    imagination;
& don't forget Venice, that murky soup of dreams . . .), it's that simple.
    No, this
Is a poem entirely about death, hmmm, about murder really. Death by
    murder,
Murder as the stage of rage, the passionate articulation of envy, desire,
    jealousy,
Despair, & cool calculation. Yet this is also a poem about style, attitude,
    blazing

164

David St. John

Panache, & white-hot courage. Puzzled yet? You should be. Because
     quite quickly
This is becoming a poem about my dead father & his own passion
     for the mystery
Novels of Chandler & Hammett, his favorite noir flicks of the Forties, &
     oh
Yeah, those S. S. Van Dine books he treasured, all that elegance a model
For me in adolescence (think of it: Van Dine, right there alongside
     prancing
Jim Morrison— go figure). It was the smoky atmospheres of sex &
     mystery
That stuck with me, from Bogart in *The Big Sleep* or *The Maltese
     Falcon*, *
Or Robert Mitchum in *Out of the Past*, all of those guys
Too cool for school, all of them beat up & grown up, wiser & older than
God himself, & even Elliott Gould in the Altman version of
     The Long Goodbye,
His clothes studiously slept in, made my father laugh out loud
Each time he said, looking sideways as he scraped a match along a
     stucco wall,
Amazed at some new absurdity in the world, "It's OK with me . . . ."
So life
Lived, my father taught me, is life darkened at the edges & made
     therefore
More luminous at its heart. As I move now so roughly into this late
     & deeply
Mysterious adulthood, jagged & reckless, cautious & desperate, so
     much of
My past life murdered in its bed, I sometimes want to be nothing,
Nothing but movement, nothing but motion, the arc of departure moving
     away
From people & things & places. I need a little more of that tough guy,
     kiss-my-
Ass nonchalance these days just to get by. That's what I think. All motion,
All moving away, away, just fucking away . . . even as the train keeps
     moving
Farther from Rome, yet always closer, closer to Florence.

*Note: My uncle Richard's favorite post-Merchant Marine story came from those years
he worked on Bogart's boat, *Santana*, & how just after clearing the breakwater out of
San Pedro, Bogart would, my uncle claimed, "whip it out & piss off the side of the
boat—a huge grin on his face, & my God that guy was hung like a horse!"

JEN HOFER

Excerpts from *From the Valley of the Death* *

"the ridge route — highway 99"

as the night softens, so the day too softens. or hardens, brittles, misfits, weeps at embankment edge, sees beyond the curved ledge of inundation to the buildings like rocks or craters below, crushed, folded in on themselves, but not folded, crumpled, deflated, airless, no space, no lift for under bird-wing, so not soft at all. gaps shaped by the between stretching from one wire to the next, one alley to another, to forgo street names or petty junctures, no unclaimed territories, markers in place, guards in place, trees mobile or could be but at this point still. we stave off the news. we can stave off the news, sipping coffee, laundering towels, avoiding idleness and ill will. through the glass is not against the glass, there is no sound, or there is sound, softly, sharply, trilling, intelligible to our other other ear, listening softly, sharply, trilling, twining out from no center as the tilt shifts softly around us but not about us.

"desert christ park — yucca valley, california"

being buffeted by the wind. not really buffeted, nudged. advised. being in an oblivion placelessly yours in progress. being fixed, stranded in a crowd of jostling airs, in an accident. not really in, by or for. accidents. the trees are being exactly like trees, only more so. birdless happenstance. being unbolted from familiarity or fabric billowing off its roll or the tracks pushed up in places from the swift below. being very still in transit. moratoriums. as if saying were a kind of erasure. being erased, remnants lift and lilies occult, the obfuscation of pleasure which is not distinguishable. being in ozone park, being stymied, being not really fixed, but skipped. being asked into exactitude by a non-anthropomorphic world. somewhere music falters and systems have been gently placed in position beneath an organic veneer under fluorescent lights. being told what to do, yet no one really doing the telling.

* *The titles of these poems come from postcards created by Merle Porter, on which the poems were originally written.*

MARY ARMSTRONG

The Shape of Light

Charlie says, "Don't move,
that steer don't like our looks."
I don't like the steer's looks either,
the way he turns his head from side to side
as if measuring the distance from there
to here, where we stand
sweating in prairie sun
that bleaches the grass yellow,
draws the sap from posts
along the barbed-wire fence.
It's pulled the sky into its heat,
scorched it bare of clouds,
of birds. Even the dark shape
of the steer takes on a kind of radiance
as if what had been animal is changed
to something terrible with light.
Its body seems to thicken, muscles
move beneath the hide like springs.
Charlie says, "Let's go," pulls me with him,
running past abandoned wells,
their pump jacks rusted motionless.
There's no shade here where paint has peeled
from tanks, their metal ladders hooked like spines.
We climb one to the top, every rung
a step away, as if we're climbing into sky,
into the furnace that is sun, afraid,
wanting only what we know
of earth, and that enough to keep us—
enough to bring us down.

Mary Armstrong

Angels Flight

The Angels Flight funicular originally
opened in Los Angeles on December 31, 1901

One A.M. The counterbalanced cars are bolted down.
In a furnished room on Clay Street, the day conductor
sleeps against the naked heat of his third wife.
He dreams the cars by name: Olivet and Sinai.
Each car holds thirty-eight—one penny
for the uphill ride, downhill is free. "Ain't, that
the truth," his wife would say.

Six A.M. Sinai lurches up, then back, then up
the grade—one minute to the top—
the "Shortest Railway in the World" ascends,
descends, three hundred twenty feet between
Hill Street and Olive.   The day conductor
rings the bell. This is the time he likes: the empty car,
its fourteen windows gray with fog, the swells asleep
on Bunker Hill beneath Victorian peaked roofs.
Below him, offices and shops, the city's five-globe
streetlights pale inside a haze, the century
on track; ascending.

Mary Armstrong

All the Possibilities

I've been thinking of my friend,
how she knotted sheets
over patio beams, jumped
into death with one snap
of her neck, as quickly as that,
the wind haunting her gown,
blowing the white cotton cloth
away from her legs, lifting it
at the shoulders as if she were
raising her arms, as if by some miracle
the body she'd slipped from
could move on its own.
I was raised on miracles,
the laying on of hands, the desperate
longing to be saved
that took mother to her knees,
pulled me with her
to the Coliseum, the Shrine,
to auditoriums where healers
in white robes, raised their arms,
shuddered in the spotlight,
in the quick intake of breath
that brought believers to the edge
of seats, leaning forward
in the dark as hope was turned
to something everyone could see,
if that was what they wanted.
And my friend, gently lowered
to the ground by strangers,
is colorless and cold to touch,
moon-streaked with shadows,
she is something now that takes my breath:
white nightgown on the grass,
the possibilities of her pale neck;
everything a miracle.

MARY FITZPATRICK

In Time of Drought

We wait for rain
here on the apron of driveway
where cats rearrange their shadows; here
on tedium's runway, blowing smoke rings
in lieu of clouds; and here
stuck on the weather channel, filling
hopeful sandbags, we wait
for a storm to move in. Rinse us,
quench us. Every plant
has gathered up its arteries
in anticipation. We could use
a deafening roar.
Our slim hopes
curl. Dear Jet Stream,
please descend. I want
a willow wand, I want
a douser – water
to plump our
withered hearts,
waiting.

ELLEN REICH

Tree, You Took Too Long to Bloom

Banana tree, you soaked up my water, crumbled my walk,
swallowed a boy, that dark night of the hit and run.
Fresh sprints of blood, lavender ooze from bruises,
abrasion of a mind stripped, barren as you, by screech of tires
that sped off, leaving a stagnant body lost in sweaty palmed
confusion. A mumble of grunts called conversation saves
the carbon dioxide between us. I wait for the boy to recover.
I wait for you to bloom.

A punishment. Your leaves should beat against my skin,
slash me until blood is blotted up by handkerchiefs,
gauze blouses, yellow-red. You sprang a mutant growth,
all size without substance, hollow. I listened to you alone,
shivering in purple wind, splitting leaves to feather.
My night companion, smooth hewn and hard trunk
to put arms around, size of a young man's waist,
smooth as his face, I rub my wishes into you.

LAUREL ANN BOGEN

I Dream the Light of Reason II

The Reasonable Woman is a hope chest, a locked cabinet.

The Reasonable Woman is pleasant enough.

The Reasonable Woman is the converse of sex.

The Reasonable Woman is a durable good, a sound diagnosis.

The Reasonable Woman is a subordinate clause.

The Reasonable Woman is childproof, although Heidi is already up to
her knee.

The Reasonable Woman is a skillet, a war bond.

The Reasonable Woman is a fugue heard on the intercom.

The Reasonable Woman is a graph of stock options, the percentage of
return.

The Reasonable Woman is open to suggestion.

The Reasonable Woman is a string bean, a cauliflower, a field of
potatoes.

The Reasonable Woman is a packet of Alka-Seltzer in the Accounts
Payable file.

The Reasonable Woman is considering bankruptcy.

The Reasonable Woman is a stacked heel, a running shoe.

The Reasonable Woman is a pair of pantyhose in the bathroom sink.

The Reasonable Woman is fat free.

The Reasonable Woman is a shadow of herself.

Why would The Reasonable Woman become unreasonable?

Laurel Ann Bogen

The Door for Love and Death

— after Tomaz Salamun

You push the shadow against the wall.
Open the door for love and death.
What rooms are rented there?

In the room of Exquisite Torture,
A woman watches her lover shave.

In the Room of Hopeless Romantic,
A man weeps before a portrait of Voltaire.

In the Room of Maternal Instinct,
The rose is embalmed.

In the Room of Amorous Adventure,
Both doors hide the tiger.

In the Room of My Life,
I give up one and love the other.

Laurel Ann Bogen

Mystery Spot with Gaze Turned Inward

What vortex pulsates above my bed?
Sprawled among the flannel sheets
and four felines waiting to be fed,
he ponders these questions of ultimate
torque and consequence.
How the little wheels of his mechanism spin!
Great is his dynamo — a nuclear reactor
whirrs in his Kenmore guarantee.

I stick to him like gravity —
an inescapable pull
impels my Volkswagen
down the 2 to the 134
hurtling past freeway exits
taco stands and mini-marts
from Highland Park to Lake Street
past the tinted windows of Roscoe's House
of Chicken and Waffles,
the Planned Parenthood clinic whose clients
cup furtive joints in the parking lot,
the Craftsman house with the blue Christmas lights
where Lil' Kim blares from the porch.
Down the street, maple leaves pile
like dunes in his marvelous yard.
There, in the melting light, I stop
to measure the turbulence,
plant herbs, calibrate our inverse polarity,
wind socks flapping in the sun, an oscillation
of simple mysteries caught then funneled outward.

DENNIS PHILLIPS

On Exile

At the first sound of motors
you must put down the axe
in this desert that's never grown a tree.

The way is set.
You curl into any cut or crevice
until the hours force shadows
and the route opens up till dawn.

This is the day of catastrophe.
The breeze that signals evening
blows grains that cover lizard tracks.
The news of motors will filter from above.

You might think that next comes fire
and with reassurance shiver in cold.

The city won't leave your ears
but even the slightest breath of wind
displaces if only temporarily
the constant frequency of your history.

Dennis Phillips

On Zygotes and Thanatos

Said the minnow to the plastic bag
no sight of the endgame, the film's the thing.

If you live long enough you find yourself
back at the memory of local history.

Said the forresta ultra naturum
to the selva oscura, lava's not our biggest worry
but it can't be ignored.

The memory of a local history's
just another way of tracing a narrative.

*

Coupled with sirens
and a mediated sense of catastrophe
only earplugs or shipwreck are viable.
Some doors abhor a vacuum.

What a misunderstanding,
the deadbolt and the windlass said,
to see magnetism as gravity
or gravity as desire.

The keys are left in the chamber,
every portal opens on a name.

In the gutter water runs clear
like the faint howling we hear
high in the background.

*

Angels abandon the keys
and collect around a bonfire
while tankers stretch their moorings,
while the ambivalent sea
springs chop and chaos.

Dennis Phillips

Tracing a narrative
while ordnance streaks a restive night
marks a moment.

Angels at the shoreline wait
signaling with fire.

*

Lights have gone off.
Angels repair to the wings.
Age hangs with different anchors
whereas the slender necks of angels
always hold their heads erect.

The marked moment the center of despair and hope.

Fond old men sing their lyrics.
The tides flood, the tides pull out.
Tired old men mend their spirits,
see angels' tides with eyes devout.

Lights off, angels gone.
One coin of age
restraint, compression
a shadow on a stage.

CECILIA WOLOCH

Why I Believed, as a Child, that People Had Sex in Bathrooms

Because they loved one another, I guessed.
Because they had seven kids and there wasn't
a door in that house that was ever locked —
except for the bathroom door, that door
with the devil's face, two horns like flame
flaring up in the grain of the wood
(or did we only imagine that shape?)
which meant the devil could watch you pee,
the devil could see you naked.
Because that's where people took off their clothes
and you had to undress for sex, I'd heard,
whatever sex was — lots of kissing and other stuff
I wasn't sure I wanted to know.
Because at night, when I was scared, I just
climbed into my parents' bed. Sometimes
other kids were there, too, and we slept
in a tangle of sheets and bodies, breath;
a full ashtray on the nightstand; our father's
work clothes hung over a chair; our mother's
damp cotton nightgown twisted around her legs.
Because when I heard babies were made from sex
and sex was something that happened in bed,
I thought: *No, the babies are already there
in the bed*. And more babies came.

Because the only door that was ever locked
was the bathroom door — those two inside
in the steam of his bath, her hairspray's mist,
because sometimes I knocked and was let in.
And my father lay in the tub, his whole dark body
under water, like some beautiful statue I'd seen.
And my mother stood at the mirror, fixing her hair,
or she'd put down the lid of the toilet
and perched there, talking to him.

Cecilia Woloch

Because maybe this was their refuge from us —
though they never tried to keep us away.
Because my mother told me once
that every time they came home from the hospital
with a brand new baby, they laughed
and fell in love all over again
and couldn't wait to start making more.
Should this have confused me? It did not.
Because I saw how he kissed the back of her neck
and pulled her, giggling, into his lap;
how she tucked her chin and looked up at him
through her eyelashes, smiling, sly.
So I reasoned whatever sex they had, they had
in the bathroom — those steamy hours
when we heard them singing to one another
then whispering, and the door stayed locked.

Because I can still picture them, languid, there,
and beautiful and young — though I had no idea
how young they were — my mother
soaping my father's back; her dark hair
slipping out of its pins ...
Because what was sex, after that? I didn't know
he would ever die, this god in a body, strong as god,
or that she would one day hang her head
over the bathroom sink to weep. I was a child,
only one of their children. Love was clean.
Babies came from singing. The devil was wood
and had no eyes.

Cecilia Woloch

East India Grill Villanelle

Across the table, Bridget sneaks a smile;
she's caught me staring past her at the man
who brings us curried dishes, hot and mild.

His eyes are blue, intensely blue, hot sky;
his hair, dark gold; his skin like cinnamon.
He speaks in quick-soft accents; Bridget smiles.

We've come here in our summer skirts, heels high,
to feast on fish and spices, garlic naan,
bare-legged in the night air, hot and mild.

And then to linger late by candlelight
in plain view of the waiter where he stands
and watches from the doorway, sneaks a smile.

I'd dress in cool silks if I were his wife.
We try to glimpse his hands — *no wedding band?*
The weather in his eyes is hot and mild.

He sends a dish of mango-flavored ice
with two spoons, which is sweet; I throw a glance
across the shady patio and smile.

But this can't go on forever, or all night
— or could it? Some eternal restaurant
of longing not quite sated, hot and mild.

And longing is delicious, Bridget sighs;
the waiter bows; I offer him my hand.
His eyes are Hindu blue and when he smiles
I taste the way he'd kiss me, hot and mild.

Cecilia Woloch

My Old True Love

My campesino,
barefoot
in the kitchen,
3 a.m.,
jeans rolled to your calves.
My sling-shot lover,
dog-shit mogul,
king of beans
and garlic, wine.
My melancholy whistler,
sleek delinquent,
darker twin.
My outlaw of the roses
through the fence.
My unplucked plum.
My *hey-young-lady* of a man.
My dear,
my love,
my shamed heart shamed.
My dirt-poor prince
among the sparrows
and the power lines,
my friend.

HOLADAY MASON

Prism

And the next day at noon, under a tree, I balance a meal on my knees
& watch midsummer leaves fall, quivering like furred caterpillars
in the grass under the cut velvet lace of shade.
One of the dead comes to sit at my right hip, explaining the facts
of forgiveness, distinct from grief, which, like trouble,
must be culled from clinging to things. My brother dead
at fifty-six with such suede brown eyes & now, the crushed organ
between my thin ribs hammering as I sit longing so badly for his
    smell.
I offer rice. He declines. *Unraveling is not unworthy of love,* he says,
exactly the way the life of music comes undone in the moment
a note flares alive, exactly like a curving candle flame, each shifting
particle dying & birthing at once. Today, between my legs is the sweet
    aching
stamp of a man not seen for months, who washed up with the moon
    tide,
coming inside the moment the round black & white clock, (whose
    face
was turned to the mirror) reflected the seconds back onto themselves
    perfectly.
Then on an arrow fine point of focus, his body, each touch, began &
    ended
its own arc, burning holy as australis borealis, strangely rare,
no matter how familiar the hue. My mouth told my heart in a dream to
    build
a wedding dress of my own skin. In broad daylight the ghost knows how
badly I failed, how badly he himself failed, how sorry, sorry sad the
hungers of lost children— hate sewn of despair. In the sunlight, the tiered
    fountain's droplets
split into bracelets of light, veils of elementals locked in union, like
    these men,
who've left some of themselves inside me— plus one sweet black
    butterfly
bruise on my inner arm, a blue tiger in the clock—purring. The dead one
begins to smile as if breaking the sound barrier. He's traveling all over
    & all at once
has decided to take a bite of my bean soup— the spoon now playing

the inside
of the clay bowl in a little clink, clink symphony, exactly in that same
   slow way
dawn collects our names through the dark hours, cradling us all in the
   pearled
petals of our dreams. A flea bites my ankle. I am a tambourine
under this tissue sky. At noon, the moon waxing, until tomorrow,
is abiding with the others, on the other side of earth, in the other day
or is it the next day or is it this same day, but midnight? I remember to
   shiver.
I shiver blue love talking to the dead one whose eyes remain the color I
   recall.
I waltz the spoon given music of this noon meal, alone with the imprint
   of one man
in my cunt, another in the grave— my flesh, a wrinkling silk dress, some
shimmering skin a snake might gradually shake off, iridescent as
   moonstone
or water, not just how bones are flutes, & dust is heaven, not that, but,
how Being floats over & within the specifics, how the body is the bowl
   & the rice—
serpent & water— echoing cave inside of which I find you again &
   again—brothers,
lovers, beloveds, all of us are there— here, always & at once...
   listen!
Can you hear? Can you hear?

PAUL VANGELISTI

Alephs Again

for Adriano Spatola (1941-1988)

A is an angel who wants absolutely nothing. She looks elegant in torn
trousers and almost never answers the phone. She seldom speaks,
especially when spoken to. Right now A's on Adriano's lap making him
laugh.

B is bothersome, even bitter sometimes, when substituted for the first
letter of your surname. Not B, you say, aping your father, V as in victory.
Both of you lack ambition.

C is a constant, not unlike chance or a comma not critically needed, or a
capital after a colon or after so many days and nights and letters and
intercontinental calls and an ecstasy still of exclamations. C definitely
lacks charity.

D is for deeds done and undone as in legend or democracy, for instance,
which you may truly love in order to destroy. Without T there isn't any
D. Ideologically speaking D is always hard.

E is easily the most equivocal letter in many European languages. A
dipping of the tongue past expectation. Especially when it's become the
first letter of your name.

F is found frequently in Finland where I'm told the major golf
tournament tees off at midnight, June 21. Or is it Iceland? Fortunately
none of us needs to find out.

G is the most generous letter in the Gnostic alphabet. Gregarious to the
extreme, he gets under his lover's skin by generally preferring an
evening around the table with friends to her whispered generalizations.
G also likes good shoes.

H, like hopelessness or history, is happily absent from this alphabet.
He's high-minded and writes criticism. H, like heart, is a commodity.

184

Paul Vangelisti

I is for the innocence I won't insist upon. I remember stopping a little boy or girl on the street, or marching into the butcher shop under our apartment to give away my favorite toy. Often something I'd pestered my mother about for weeks. I tried to write an entire book once without I.

J is just how I feel after the rain starts, sitting at a window. Or maybe more like judging somebody you don't like, jumping to a conclusion jabbed from the jetsam of self-hate which, in a certain season, juts from the lagoon of your joyless life. Not even the dead believe any of this. Stop the bus.

K is king in the knowledge that a kingdom demands the killing of its sovereign. Or else K is tired of waiting in the Caffé Canova, watching two elderly German ladies consume a plateful of sandwiches they told the waiter they didn't care for. K is a great kidder, if sometimes a little unkind.

L lingers from the other alphabet, a platitude abandoned, a leak from the other side. L wants nobody except maybe some angels, Uncle Bob, his son, T, and his daughter, S, I who got married and seldom talks to on the telephone, and now and again a few dead friends. L certainly never felt good about himself.

M means all that has mattered, whom you've loved and left out of this alphabet. M's also the man you will never be. Oh well.

N isn't for the novel not written, not those poems Nevin would never show me. N is a hero who knocks out the eye of the monster and beholds a long-legged Nausicaa orient among the waves.

O, incidentally, has no private life, what others call a 'life of one's own.' From the desk O sees a little man operate a power mower for a minute or so up and down a patch of lawn. Soon O's tall blond neighbor, in red heels as usual, occupies the street with her stride. O is pleased.

P is for politics, the art of pretending to have some power over life. Others are necessary to play. All are expected to have plenty of persistence, some ambition and a winning pleasure. The dead are no good at it. Only children are ill-prepared for politics, until they produce families of their own. Particularly when they think they need to be loved.

Q is unquestionably the queerest letter in the alphabet. When's the last time, for instance, you quoted somebody from Quito? Maybe my tall blond neighbor, who's Spanish-speaking, is from Ecuador. That would qualify her disdain.

R seems always reasonable. Even when he's never eaten there before. Recently, he tends to make a strong impression. But who knows? Life's irregular that way. At 3:38 this morning a rather strong earthquake kept R awake for almost an hour waiting for the aftershock. Which of us, after all, can truly rise to the occasion?

Somebody said S is the most overused sound in English poetry. I lisped as a boy so they slit the fraenum under my tongue and sent me to speech lessons on Saturdays. Even if the face of the earth shook, how soon and sentimental depends on the depth of the quake. It seems hard to consider any name but Simone for my daughter.

T is temporarily charismatic, a capital of tenderness. Above it teeter all the excuses you've ever invented. T makes you do things you daren't because there might not be another time. T is the letter, amid a whisper of dashes, the man upstairs most regrets. T plays the odds. T always takes time. T is one of my son's names.

Unless U is unquenchable rich men will unearth the kingdom of heaven. He sees a fat boy urge a foot off the curb to scurry across the street under his mother's eye. U as usual feels unfulfilled when he's more likely undone. He's never yelled, "Kill the umpire!"

Very little varies. Vain resentment then some vague acceptance of a vainglorious life. So much for verisimilitude or the Uncle Fred you were threatened with too virulently becoming. No longer the victorious V coached by your dad, the fervor of the almost bitten lip, but now come south to lazy empire, the late vowels and the weakened stops, where not only all the ladders start but your name too, as in bad, band, bang and bank.

W's always been a mystery. The complement of mother or a waltz in the waves. Either way sounds windy and not much to do with women or writing. Little's got to do with writing. Maybe whisky, maybe not.

X is too imposing for words. There's only one under X in my thesaurus, X-shaped, and that too chiasmal.

Y I've always heard as a question: whether in the female attitude just yielding enough or upside down standing as a man in all too simple yearning. The Greek *I* it's called in Italian. Yes is, in fact, more like it.

Z is much closer to the start than you ever imagined. She stands apart, on nobody's lap. If anything you'd love to lay your bitter head on hers. If she speaks it's right out of the top of her forehead. Or so it seems, Z, not X, marks the spot.

REX WILDER

The boomerang is a four-line poem in which the first word or sound rhymes with the last. The first line is the toss, the second the outward trajectory, the third the return, the fourth the catch.

Four Boomerangs

WASTED)

Wasted
display pastries make me want to get out
more — to be inhaled, handled,
and tasted.

BLOG)

Blog
entry: Every day, the poet walks
a different invisible
dog.

SOME)

Some
view! Press me into it; ask
the camera to be
a thumb.

ROMANCE)

Romance
on a plate. A foil ballerina wears the Ice Cube Prince
for shoes. He melts, *has to*, for her
to dance.

MICHELLE BITTING

Black Guitar

To pick that glint-edged glamour,
lacquered body, lustrous odalisque,
strung flower. Imagine skipping
my fingers like Dorothy
down its long fretted neck,
enchanted path, inevitable Oz,
the O of sound spinning wild
from that midnight pit. Big obsidian
lung sighing, Billie Holiday's
sheened hip if a hip could sing
and hers could. Every pore
pitch perfect. Notes embossed
on the underside of skin. Even
nostrils, an interior syrup,
run through with primordial
song. I crave this instrument
with cut-away puzzle, missing
curlicue and plug-in potentials.
The way I crave salvation,
a head-long plunge
into amplified abyss, a certain
grunge such beauty requires.
Three squares humiliation
and a stomach for the fall.
Patience, patience. My singing
improves with every hard knock
plucked. Into these arms, Takamine,
my dream true come — strapped on,
tuned up, Lover Man, locomotive,
on your dark-strummed rails
we're forever born to run.

Morning, Highway 126

Farmers heft and truckers load crates of lemons
onto flatbeds at first light.
The skillet trees stream past,
silhouettes of yellow fruit and shadowed green
like something aquatic. Here I go,
sucked under, again. I love what won't
belong to me
and so sit tight, fingering
the wound, the open sinew,
sticky gem pot
in the lap of the matter.
At any moment, my heart a bowl
of pabulum, stirred or eaten.
Flimsy houses whiz by
the flanks of my eyes, jimmied
plank to dust
by the cranks of decline.
I drive while reason takes a hike.
Let me spin, I say.
Let me crumble in your hands,
my raw materials, my soil
ganged up on. You
and your gorgeous worms
that won't stop working on it.

KIM DOWER

Extraction

My dentist tells me it's the longest root
he's ever seen as he uses all his strength
to pull out my top back molar been hurting
since as long as I can remember feels like he's
extracting my brain forcing every thought
I ever had out of my head longest root he said
my mouth so numb I have no mouth
the tooth doesn't want to leave its warm
dysfunctional socket headquarters from where
it's been tormenting me for years lighthouse of pain
tooth that reminds me everyday that everything's
not okay let me see its calcified pulp let me roll it
in my fingers remember being a girl alone
in the dentist's waiting room reading stories
in *Newsweek* about the soldiers coming home
man on the moon get the tooth out remove
this neon time bomb red alert tooth depleting
my good will let me worship it for showing me
what hurts can be removed will end let me
wear it around my neck to prove even roots
can be ripped out

Kim Dower

Boob Job

Trying on clothes in the backroom
of Loehmann's, a stranger invites me
to feel her breasts, a stranger trying on
dresses that don't fit and I can see
her breasts are larger than they want
to be, and she can see I'm watching,
asks me to help zip her up and I struggle
to pull her in, smooth out her sunburned skin,
tug, ask her to shake herself in, she tells me
she just got them, didn't know they'd come out
so big isn't sure she likes them, not even her
husband cares, he's not a breast man, she says,
he's an ass man *but I'm not getting an ass job,*
good, I say, because how do you even *get* an ass job,
do you want to feel them, she asks, and I do, *so* I do
and they feel like bean bags you'd toss at a clown's face
at a kid's party, I squeeze them both at the same time,
cup my hands underneath them, she says, *go ahead,*
squeeze some more, it's not sexual, aren't they heavy,
I don't want to have them around every day, her nipples
headlights staring into the dressing room mirror, red scars
around their circumferences, angry circles I want to run
my finger around, *you should have seen them before*
I had them lifted, they were long drooping points,
couldn't stand looking at them anymore, can I see yours,
so I show her, so small hers could eat mine alive,
nipples like walnuts, do you think I should make mine
bigger, and there we are examining one another's boobs,
touching, talking about them like they aren't there,
don't matter, forgetting how it felt when we were twelve
or thirteen, one morning when they first appeared
sore, swollen, exciting, new, when they had the power
to turn us into women we no longer knew.

AUSTIN STRAUS

If I Were A Wall

there'd be obscenities,
political slogans
and initials of dead lovers
scrawled in red and yellow,
blue, green and black
along my belly

and I'd hold birds of
paradise and ravens and
sparrows and all the wrens
and robins of the universe
and they'd sing and feed
and build nests and paint poems
down my sides with their shit

if I were a wall

and if I were a wall
I'd hold back the floods
and keep out the stampeding
cattle but allow every
horse to jump me and I'd
amble slowly among
houses and let my
stones mumble hymns
while the farmers slept

if I were a wall

and if I were a wall
I'd be hard and winding
as a frozen river
or soft and deadly
as a sleeping cobra
or in my meanderings
I'd be a story

Austin Straus

written in sibilants
and curliques

if I were a wall

and if I were a wall
I'd let myself tumble into fragments
to be dug up and buried in museums
or be carved into faces that are
worshipped at midnight by
moondriven witches

if I were a wall

and I'd refuse the weight
of corpses or the smack
of noon sun or gouging
by bullets or wailing of
mourners or anything but
warm drizzles and tall grass
brushing my thighs

if I were a wall

and I'd dream of entering myself
and becoming a suite of rooms
multiplying and dividing,
turning and turning
until I was an infinite cavern
all chiaroscuro and texture
where unfettered dreams
could wander in search of
unsuspecting dreamers

if I were a wall

Austin Straus

Even Paranoids
(in memoriam Delmore Schwartz)

Shadowed by shadows, stared at
by strangers. Silence on the phone
definitely not God's.
CIA? FBI? IRS?
Some crazed ex-girlfriend
obsessed with my number?
Eyes in the wallpaper, ears
among blossoms. Ex-wives gossip
in their memoirs, peddle diaries
for bucks. Babbled about on
talk shows/giggles and smirks.
Former lovers fire darts at my
photos. I'm the villain in nightmares,
my son's hairy monster.
Even the ocean keeps shushing
my name. Late at night, far away,
the insistent yowling of cats.
That which I'd rather keep secret
found lipsticked in toilets, scrawled
across skies. Crows mock my
excuses, curs mimic my lies.
I'm riddled by missiles shot by
unerring tongues. Mind Swiss-cheesy
with holes, brain leaking self-esteem.
An inner homunculus screeches curses
at this so-mangled existence. I turn
from the face that uglies at me
when I shave. Who's driving this
hearse, stealing my lines, rasping
through my lips words I don't
recognize? Can I trust my next move
or anything I say? What the fuck
am I up to? I'm the wrong one to ask.

Even I'm out to get me.

L.A. Morning

Maybe it's Ian. Maybe walking with him
to the sitter's, a kind of
religious exercise, his singing
counterpoint to mine as we walk
wakens the gods.
The fog dances more gently
into the trees. This ripest of
moments gives birth to amazement
so pure it hurts. That the world
arranges itself so vividly before me!
That all things, trees, houses,
weeds, stones, roses,
even porched pigeons and a flat
gray sky, everything
glows! And my woman loves me
and my son adores me
and these marvels were set out for us to
stroll through and for one sweet minute
I have absolutely nothing to regret.

MEHNAZ SAHIBZADA

Damsel Ghost

Every city girl could use a boat.
       And a lake. And an empty
afternoon to sail out west. Which is why

I put on the white dress, the one I'd
       bought at an estate sale,
grabbed my childhood quilt, and brushed

my hair till it shook. I hung a lantern
       on the prow and let the winds
lead the way. Nobody knew I was

fleeing. I'd tossed my cell away
       in the laundry pile, my flip-flops
in the sink. No I wasn't drunk.

I didn't drink. But I'd been looking
       at these pictures of swans
all morning, wishing I'd been

born with a longer neck. Someone
       who could freely drift
up the coast. Someone who didn't

live on cigarettes and toast. But here
       I was, escaping the magic monotony
of my life. No one's wife, no one's mother.

Just a damsel ghost. The trees hung gray.
       The sun a shadowed eye blinking.
The good news was the boat drifted long,

didn't sink. And I felt tall and wild—
       three candles lit. My breathing
slowed. I was miles from L.A. The day

was water, mountains, air, and I'd escaped.
          No insight came, but this I knew:
Every city girl could use a boat. A white

dress and a lake. And an afternoon quilted
          with gold thread, after a morning
in bed staring at photographs of swans.

Muse Noir

Every time I write, I sense his hand sliding
up my thigh. Blackening each metaphor, he hammers
my good-girl past until it shatters like a glass mug.

I can't shrug him away. One night in Lahore
when I was fifteen, he climbed beside me in bed,
fastened a palm around my wrist. It was the only

time I saw his face, the square brown chin
and espresso-stained grin, the cunning smile that
colonized my head. I said, when I get back

to California, I'll grind you up like a bean. But
he just waved a palm-sized cross and proposed.
I said yes, of course. Still he stood me up

for prom. I wore the ruby dress with the side
slit and waited on the porch. Waited and waited
until my thoughts took off their heels and like a corpse

stood still. For months he did not show. I spent
the evenings sketching black tulips, drinking coffee–
the café the one place he was likely to be–the air

prayer-whipped with the nuns who liked to visit,
play chess in the corner. There the lighting was
lunar. One night, reading a ghost story in the back,

my thoughts woke electric. I put on lipstick,
pressed it on even too. His hand gripped my neck.
The fear delicious, the joy rose up so fast,

I couldn't move. If I stay, he said,
you'll carry delusions, make mad like
Edgar Allen Poe. I told him I wasn't the kind

of girl who wanted a rose. He laughed at my quiver,
handed me a silver ring, something gothic. We
didn't kiss. It would have been uncouth

with the nuns watching. But the verdict
was in. My conscience mugged by a thief, I was
wife to spinning dark, to gunfire on the street.

MICHAEL C FORD

Marie Windsor

Remembering her, always,
as the quintessential brunette
femme fatale: even in her
crossover to 1960s television
when she, still, in series reruns
moves across the silver screen
like 125 pounds of warm fog

She always essayed the kinds of
women who were these troublemakers
on *The Untouchables* or perpetrators
on *The Rifleman* or murder victims on
Perry Mason: a woman, then, who kept
reinventing herself, as a counterpoint
of feminine infinities: even, with
intense considerations directed
towards Belle Starr lady outlaw
equestrian buckskin barometer

She walks us through decrepit rooms
reinforcing evil or in a bad place of a
Narrow Margin, where *The Sniper*
draws his envious bead

I admired her most, when she essayed
 a rocket scientist from East St. Louis
and convivially commiserating with
Cat Women of the Moon

And the sultry sound her lush voice
makes is velvet stretched across
a field of gravel.

STEVE GOLDMAN

The Lone Ranger Goes to War

Lone Ranger or no, the Lone Ranger is drafted
      into the Army.
Because of his mythical, trans-temporal character, he serves
        simultaneously in WWI, WWII, Korea, Viet Nam and the
        Persian Gulf.
Forbidden his costume, mask and silver Colts,
He is issued a regulation uniform and weapon,
      and
denied his request to serve at his obvious Military Occupational
        Specialty –
That of scout or sniper, employing his legendary marksmanship
        to shoot the guns from the enemy's hands, effectively but
        harmlessly.
There is no talk of that here. Here people get shot in the balls.

Being the Lone Ranger, he further requests that he be made
Commanding General, so he won't have to take any orders,
Or the lowliest private so he won't have to give any.
Naturally, he is made a captain of infantry.

He strives to shield his men from the worst insane excesses of his
        superiors,
while obeying the orders of these superiors leavened by such reason as
        can be mustered in combat.
Being the Archetypal Loyal American,
he vigorously prosecutes
        The War Against the Enemy,
Only now for once, he cannot adhere to his
prime value of never killing anyone.

Like so many who had gone before him,
he emerges from the war mad,
or at least greatly saddened for life.

RD ARMSTRONG

While Reading Lorca

Always I am thinking of you
even at the oddest times
alone in the house
washing dishes
or taking a leak
while reading a book
or watching the news
or watching the gutters
turn red
first with rust
and then with blood
while reading Lorca
or Yeats
or Bukowski
listening to the blues or
listening to my friends
bantering
or conversations overheard
at a bar
or a cafe
you are just around the corner
rushing into
and through my life
on your way to somewhere else.

RD Armstrong

Corazon

The walking stick,
leaning in the corner, knows it.
And, so do I: the wanderlust
beckons.

Soon enough -
you're silhouette in the doorway,
slipping my embrace,
the long shadow,
the creaking of the gate,
the final wave from the crest
of the hill.

The wind that whistles
through the treetops
will bring nothing
but the memory
of your sighs.
Though I search the sky
for a message, I will
find only clouds,
feathers and dust,
pale light and a hint of winter
(no trace of you).

Now it begins
this season of long shadows
and the silence of stone.

GAIL WRONSKY

Beneath the Ganges Where it is Dark

there is no edge.

No edge of petal.

No tin edge of star.

Without edges

there is no vividness.

This is what I

enjoy most about

being here.

Edges pretend that

one thing ends.

But nothing does end—

not here

beneath the Ganges

where it is dark.

Gail Wronsky

Clearer than amber gliding over stones

is the sunlight of thought. Quieter than the crisp fiction of
    windlessness—
Production, consumption—

aren't you tired of convincing people you're not trying to convince them
    of anything?
I am. Soil is necessary. Perhaps we could agree on that—

and stop cupping our hands beneath dry sky as if we knew what we
    wanted.
A name for what it is that happens in our minds when we're ecstatic and
    alone. When

briefly destiny uncries, like someone in a movie weeping backward.
Perhaps nothing can trump the rose of this mind-writhing (not even

the final, sealing hush of golden Buddha).
Perhaps we're trapped innately, gnat-like, in the middle of great vacant
    signs.

Perhaps we just think we are.

Gail Wronsky

Go On, Sure, Why Not

My beloved black bamboo seems wrong
today here next to the live oak on my
terrace. Though as I say that I know it's
what I've said each time I've arrived at
this precise moment, before I pause then
notice a tribe of red ants stuck like dried
blood bits in thin cracks in the oak bark. To
go on, at that point, always seems an inadequate
description of what it is we do when
Brahma wakes. Even *living* fails to describe
this inhabiting of eternity in which we
pause occasionally and insist upon staking claim
to an aesthetic point of view. *One wants
to be singled out.* At the same time, one
wants to be hidden in a thicket of sharp
black leaves to be nothing
but a pair of orange eyes without
the human burden of self-awareness. Pure fear
pure hunger pure procreant urge pure
thoughtless push. When Hamlet says *My
thoughts be bloody or be nothing worth* he's
thinking too of the grave where there is
no thinking blood no bloody thinking.

CATHIE SANDSTROM

Standing Up in a Slim Boat

after a line by Tomas Tranströmer

Freed from not knowing where you are,
I've traded the nagging worry for a shroud.

In the slim boat of each day, I stand
wary, look across the still surface.

Balance is all. The undercurrent, strong.
Not the peace I hoped for, this calm.

Cathie Sandstrom

Releasing the Birds

Next to her embroidered lawn handkerchiefs
my mother's empty gloves lay
paired in the nest of her drawer:

short white Easter ones that stopped at the wrist;
netted crocheted gloves for summer; an ecru pair
four inches past her watchband, the backs detailed

with three rows of stitching raised like fine bones;
three-quarter length pigskin to wear under coats;
black lace for cocktails, white for weddings;

sexy gloves with gathers up the length so they'd
look like they were slouching; the knitted
Bavarians, Loden green, stiff as boiled wool.

My first prom dress—strapless, floor-length—I wore
her formal opera gloves. Pearl buttons on the delicate
underside of my wrists, then the white went up and up.

I kept six pairs, my sister took the rest. Saying
someone should use them, she gave them away
at work, set them out for the taking.

Tonight, I lay the table with my mother's china.
At each place, a pair of gloves palms up, wrists
touching in a gesture of receiving and giving.

I held back the gloves she'd bought in Italy: black
leather, elbow length, the right glove torn at thumb
and palm as if she'd reached for something too late
or held onto something too long.

SHARON VENEZIO

College Essay

Is it just that I'm leaving home or has my bedroom always been this beautiful? My walls are earthy green. A black and white print of Audrey Hepburn hangs above the piano, magazine faces stare out from the closet wall, and there are words sketched in sharpie on my desk; each space a contradiction. I can't draw, but if I could for my mother a sketch of Van Gogh's Almond Blossoms with their soft hesitant life for all her looking inward, and for my father a picture of a red fronted macaw perched on the cliffs of Bolivia for all his looking outward.

My brother is a Buddhist. He's 23, says he will soon live in the forest in Sri Lanka, like a monk. He will name flowers, then unname them. He will not contact our mother. The bird in his heart does not feel hunger; it closes its soundless wings and dreams. He doesn't like his ego, tries to kill it nightly in his room. My ego would like to go to your college. I will call my mother every day. One day I will visit Sri Lanka, find my brother sitting somewhere in the Sri Pada wilderness, bring him food, tell him all I have learned at your college. He will tell me to forget it all, and I will.

Sharon Venezio

Psychology 402: Brain and Behavior

When I discover I have to dissect a sheep's brain,
I go down the hall to Animal Behavior and plead my case,
but it's too late. I'll have to pry my way through
the four ventricles, push pins into gray matter and breathe
formaldehyde through a useless white mask.

I hold the brain in my awful hands, make an incision
at the base of the cerebellum, place a red pin
into the pineal gland, a green pin into the amygdala:
here's where it feels joy, here's where it feels fear,
here's where it remembers the beautiful dying stars.

JUDITH PACHT

Bird

A slice of sheep cheese with apple

you were saying
when the window shook

— or was it the whole wall —
and on the ground a wren,

beak and needle talons
in barest motion,

obsidian eyes
dazed, fooled by light

seeming air, seeming
endless as sky.

Who hasn't flown
too fast and high,

song full
in the belly

sun-warm after a rain,
the sweet taste

dazzling. Sometimes
it ends this way,

a blind fracture
after a moment

of so much
so complete,

that fullness under
wild-streaked feathers.

Feel her, she's still warm.

CAROL V. DAVIS

Marshland

We are all intruders here
      though we fool ourselves this late winter day,
carving a place on the banks
         to anchor our heels.
We stretch over the water, hoping
        to slip onto the wings of a Great Blue Heron
but afraid to get caught in the trap of reeds, twisting
         in the foul water.
The marsh ignites: will o'wisps,
sprites, a wisp of flames,
torches held aloft by villagers
      marching on the manor.
We've read too many fairytales
        but this much is true:
I heard voices.
      Not the call of a willet or clapper rail
but a child caught beneath the ceiling of water
        the thin reed of its voice
rising in the brackish light.

NAN HUNT

I invoke you, almost deadly birds of the soul…
Duino Elegies, Rainer Maria Rilke

Wilderness Pond at Dusk

Have you been there
      when the day was one
      long basso profundo
      tone of murk and mystery?
The solitariness no one can solve.

Heard then a high note
      pitching a signal above you
      which repeats and fades
      then sharply sings again?

And you gaze up to see bowling pin
      silhouettes rolling across the sky
      pale blue to steel, clouds
      like smokey pavilions.

Briefly, dense mountains behind
      them, absorb the flying shapes.
In the clear again, they reconnoiter
      the pond. You stand very still.

Ducks come plummeting around you
      one flock then another.
A windstorm of wings. Webbed
      toes fan out to skid the air.

They stall against gravity
      until their bodies intuit the surface
      then splash down heavily.
Such awkward angels! Surely they came
      to make you smile.

Nan Hunt

Feathers return to intricate
        pleats, they hide rubbery feet
        under black water, ruddering
        to inward music, a serene wedge
        toward reeds and cattails.

One bird, sensing the slightest
        shift from an object it thought
        was a boulder, jets upward in alarm.

A cautionary urge spreads contagion
        as one whole squadron lifts abruptly
        flies and circles. And another catches
        the fear that disrupts the air.

And then the rest. You cannot belong.
You are the danger they don't know –
        don't want proven.
You swallow the call-note of your dark
        sobbing and turn again to yearning
        like a stone.

B.H. FAIRCHILD

A Starlit Night

All over America at this hour men are standing
by an open closet door, slacks slung over one arm,
staring at wire hangers, thinking of taxes
or a broken faucet or their first sex: the smell
of back-seat Naugahyde, the hush of a maize field
like breathing, the stars rushing, rushing away.

And a woman lies in an unmade bed watching
the man she has known twenty-one, no,
could it be? twenty-two years, and she is listening
to the polonaise climbing up through radio static
from the kitchen where dishes are piled
and the linoleum floor is a great, gray sea.

It's the A-flat polonaise she practiced endlessly,
never quite getting it right, though her father,
calling from the darkened TV room, always said,
"Beautiful, kiddo!" and the moon would slide across
the lacquered piano top as if it were something
that lived underwater, something from far below.

They both came from houses with photographs,
the smell of camphor in closets, board games
with missing pieces, sunburst clocks in the kitchen

that made them, each morning, a little sad.

They didn't know what they wanted, every night,

every starlit night of their lives, and now they have it.

The Invisible Man

We are kids with orange Jujubes stuck to our chins

and licorice sticks snaking out of our jeans pockets,

and we see him, or rather don't see him, when the bandages

uncoil from his face and lo, there's nothing between

the hat and the suit. It is wonderful, this pure nothing,

but we begin to be troubled by the paradoxes of non-existence

(Can he pee? If he itches, can he scratch? If he eats

Milk Duds, do they disappear?). Sure, standing around

in the girls' locker room unobserved or floating erasers

in math class, who could resist, but the enigma

of sheer absence, the loss of the body, of *who we are,*

continues to grind against us even into the Roy Rogers

western that follows. The pungent Vista Vision embodiments

of good and evil—this clear-eyed young man with watermelon

voice and high principles, the fat, unshaven dipshits

with no respect for old ladies or hard-working Baptist

farmers—none of this feels quite solid anymore. Granted,

it's the world as the world appears, but *provisional* somehow,

a shadow, a ghost, dragging behind every rustled cow

or runaway stagecoach, and though afterwards the cloud

of insubstantiality lifts and fades as we stroll out

216

B.H. Fairchild

grimacing into the hard sunlight, there is that
slight tremble of dejá-vu years later in Philosophy 412
as Professor Caws mumbles on about essence and existence,
being and nothingness, and *Happy Trails to You* echoes
from the far end of the hall.
                              In *The Invisible Man*
sometimes we could see the thread or thin wire that lifted
the gun from the thief's hand, and at the Hearst mansion
only days ago a sign explained that the orchestra
of Leonard Slye entertained the zillionaire and his Hollywood
friends on spring evenings caressed by ocean breezes
and the scent of gardenias. You can almost see them swaying
to *Mood Indigo* or *Cherokee*, champagne glasses in hand:
Chaplin, Gable, Marion Davies, Herman Mankiewicz,
and cruising large as the Titanic, William Randolph Hearst,
Citizen Kane himself. Leonard Slye sees this, too, along with
the Roman statuary and rare medieval tapestries, and thinks,
someday, someday, and becomes invisible so that he
can appear later as Roy Rogers and make movies in
Victorville, California, where Mankiewicz and Orson Welles
will write the story of an enormous man who misplaced
his childhood and tried to call it back on his death-bed.
O Leonard Slye, lifting Roy's six-gun from its holster,
O Hearst, dreaming of Rosebud and raping the castles of Europe,
O America, with your dreams of money and power,
small boys sit before your movie screens invisible
to themselves, waiting for the next episode, in which they
stumble blind into daylight and the body of the world.

B.H. Fairchild

Rave On

. . . *wild to be wreckage forever*.
James Dickey, "Cherrylog Road"

Rumbling over caliche with a busted muffler,
radio blasting Buddy Holly over Baptist wheat fields,
Travis screaming out *Prepare ye the way of the Lord*
at jackrabbits skittering beneath our headlights,
the Messiah coming to Kansas in a flat-head Ford
with bad plates, the whole high plains holding its breath,
night is fast upon us, lo, in these the days of our youth,
and we were hell on wheels, or thought we were. Boredom
grows thick as maize in Kansas, heavy as drill pipe
littering the racks of oil rigs where in summer boys
roustabout or work on combine crews north as far
as Canada. The ones left back in town begin
to die, dragging main street shit-faced on 3.2 deer
and banging on the whorehouse door in Garden City
where the ancient madam laughed and turned us down
since we were only boys and she knew our fathers.
We sat out front spitting Red Man and scanned a landscape
flat as Dresden: me, Mike Luckinbill, Billy Heinz,
and Travis Doyle, who sang, *I'm gonna live fast,*
love hard, and die young. We had eaten all the life
there was in Seward County but hungry still, hauled ass
to old Arkalon, the ghost town on the Cimarron
that lay in half-shadow and a scattering of starlight,

and its stillness was a kind of death, the last breath
of whatever in our lives was ending. We had drunk there
and tossed our bottles at the walls and pissed great arcs
into the Kansas earth where the dust groweth hard
and the clods cleave fast together, yea, where night yawns
above the river in its long, dark dream, above
haggard branches of mesquite, chicken hawks scudding
into the tree line, and moon-glitter on caliche
like the silver plates of Coronado's treasure
buried all these years, but the absence of treasure,
absence of whatever would return the world
to the strangeness that as children we embraced
and recognized as *life*. *Rave on.*

                                        Cars are cheap
at Roman's salvage strewn along the fence out back
where cattle graze and chew rotting fabric from the seats.
Twenty bucks for spare parts and a night in the garage
could make them run as far as death and stupidity
required—on Johnson Road where two miles of low shoulders
and no fence line would take you up to sixty, say,
and when you flipped the wheel clockwise, you were there
rolling in the belly of the whale, belly of hell,
and your soul fainteth within you for we had seen it done
by big Ed Ravenscroft who said you would go in a boy
and come out a man, and so we headed back through town
where the marquee of the Plaza flashed CREATURE FROM
THE BLACK LAGOON in storefront windows and the Snack Shack

where we had spent our lives was shutting down and we
sang *rave on, it's a crazy feeling* out into the night
that loomed now like a darkened church, and sang loud
and louder still for we were sore afraid.
                                        Coming up
out of the long tunnel of cottonwoods that opens onto
Johnson Road, Travis with his foot stuck deep into the soul
of that old Ford *come on, Bubba, come on* beating
the dash with his fist, hair flaming back in the wind
and eyes lit up by some fire in his head that I
had never seen, and Mike, iron Mike, sitting tall
in back with Billy, who would pick a fight with anything
that moved but now hunched over mumbling something
like a prayer, as the Ford lurched on spitting
and coughing but then smoothing out suddenly fast
and the fence line quitting so it was open field, then,
then, I think, we were butt-deep in regret and a rush
of remembering whatever we would leave behind—
Samantha Dobbins smelling like fresh laundry,
light from the movie spilling down her long blonde hair,
trout leaping all silver and pink from Black Bear Creek,
the hand of my mother, I confess, passing gentle
across my face at night when I was a child—oh, yes,
it was all good now and too late, too late, trees blurring
past and Travis wild, popping the wheel, oh too late
too late

B.H. Fairchild

and the waters pass over us the air thick
as mud slams against our chests though turning now
the car in its slow turning seems almost graceful
the frame in agony like some huge animal groaning
and when the wheels leave the ground the engine cuts loose
with a wail thin and ragged as a bandsaw cutting tin
and we are drowning breathless heads jammed against
our knees and it's a thick swirling purple nightmare
we cannot wake up from for the world is turning too
and I hear Billy screaming and then the whomp
sick crunch of glass and metal whomp *again back window*
popping loose and glass exploding someone crying out
tink tink of iron on iron overhead and then at last
it's over and the quiet comes
                                        Oh so quiet. Somewhere
the creak and grind of a pumping unit. Crickets.
The tall grass sifting the wind in a mass of whispers
that I know I'll be hearing when I die. And so
we crawled trembling from doors and windows borne out
of rage and boredom into weed-choked fields barren
as Golgotha. Blood raked the side of Travis's face
grinning rapt, ecstatic. Mike's arm was hanging down
like a broken curtain rod, Billy kneeled, stunned,
listening as we all did to the rustling silence
and the spinning wheels in their sad, manic song
as the Ford's high beams hurled their crossed poles of light
forever out into the deep and future darkness. *Rave on.*

221

B.H. Fairchild

I survived. We all did. And then came the long surrender,

the long, slow drifting down like young hawks riding on

the purest, thinnest air, the very palm of God

holding them aloft so close to something hidden there,

and then the letting go, the fluttering descent, claws

spread wide against the world, and we become, at last,

our fathers. And do not know ourselves and therefore

no longer know each other. Mike Luckinbill ran a Texaco

in town for years. Billy Heinz survived a cruel divorce,

remarried, then took to drink. But finally last week

I found this house in Arizona where the brothers

take new names and keep a vow of silence and make

a quiet place for any weary, or lost, passenger

of earth whose unquiet life has brought him there,

and so, after vespers, I sat across the table

from men who had not surrendered to the world,

and one of them looked at me and looked into me,

and I am telling you there was *a fire in his head*

and his eyes were coming fast down a caliche road,

and I knew this man, and his name was Travis Doyle.

MITCHELL UNTCH

Dear Betty Blythe Francis

I'm guessing that you are the same Betty Blythe Francis I knew in
     college
at Indiana University in Bloomington in the late 1960's and early 1970's.

I'm guessing that you are the same Betty Blythe Francis I drove home to
     Wabash
occasionally to spend a weekend with your parents on my way home to
     Fort Wayne

to visit mine. I'm guessing that you are the same Bettye Blythe Francis I
     first met
on a weekend in August of 1965 forty-eight years ago driving, to
     Bloomington to see

the opera "Carmen" with Hal Brown, whom I worked with at Camp Big
     Island
where our Boy Scout troop stayed that year and almost baked for the
     heat.

I'm guessing that there are not that many Betty Blythe Francises around
     still living,
and so I'm taking a chance that you are that same person. I'm guessing
     you're the

Betty Blythe Francis who befriended me, and I'm writing this now
     because we're
both getting older and I've been thinking about you for about forty eight
     years

and wondering how it happened that we lost contact with one another
and how the years flew by and how I never said to you the things

I'm saying to you now—what you meant to me, how much I loved
     you—
as I sit at my kitchen table and look out over the street and listen to
     birds think.

Mitchell Untch

I see you standing near the campus library as I last remember you,
    holding your
books, one hand blocking the sun from your eyes, your long shadow on
    the lawn

spinning and turning color, the leaves falling as they did every year, as
    they're doing
now, effortlessly, and the sudden wind with all its memories curling the
    lip

of your dress, tousling the tips of your hair, remembering how when I
    left
Bloomington in August of 1975 to move to California, it was sudden—

not planned—the alertness of it, and how I had temporarily lost my mind
over another boy, ignored my friends and not remembering if I said
    goodbye

or if we were on good terms or bad at that point or if we had just drifted
    apart,
as is so often the case with friendships, with love, running aground as I
    was,

so much trying to catch up on things, things I thought significant—
    furniture,
a new coffee maker, what to keep, what to throw away—not
    understanding

that everything I was leaving behind was what I needed to take with me,
    the nights
we spent on the steps of the dorm, gossip from our mouths rising like
    smoke,

each looking up at the brightness of the moon as only someone our
    age could see it,
the white flame of it in the darkness, in the winter, the morning,
    when the sun

rose, and we both stood beautiful in the earth's ease, in her bright blaze
    of color,
our shadows disappearing in the simple way that two people disappear
    into life.

224

Remember the Great Lakes? We thought they were oceans. I'm guessing you're
    still there, because I need to remember you as I knew you then, feeling
    the wind.

I'd like to think that our time here on this earth is ultimately undisturbed,
    that when
we enter it, it closes behind us, a place without despair, a beginning, an
    endlessness

played: October, the maple's red hands, spring rain signing the grass,
    and the two of us
still alive in this world, tucking in bed sheets, somewhere laughing,
    laughing like waves.

Mitchell Untch

Coming Out

To My Mother

I sat at the table
in the full light of the kitchen
while mother stood peeling
apples at the sink.
The oven was on high
and all the windows, wide open.
A fan whirred in the background.
I wanted to turn it off
so I could hear her better,
like when she whispered
"They have a cure for what you have."
I was twelve years old.
She made a sandwich
and set it down in front of me
along with some milk.
Sliding my finger
down the chilled glass,
I drew a circle on the table
and made a little pond.
"May I be excused?" I asked.
It was getting late and
I wanted to be outside
where the birds were,
where they could not be reached.
"May I?"
"Yes," she said.
She untied her apron.
She hung her silence on the door.

To My Father

We were sitting on the front porch
and he'd asked me for a smoke.
The air that night was cold.
Our breath hovered between us.

226

Mitchell Untch

Cigarette ashes drizzled
down the front of his shirt, tapered off.
I told him sometime after mother
had gone upstairs, had gone to bed.
He said, "I love you" and "anyway,"
looked out over the lawn, flicked his
cigarette butt onto the ground
and went inside.
The next day, I studied
how birds built their nests
from broken limbs and lawn scraps,
how they lifted them
into the tree's dark heart
and made them habitable.
I loved my father in his handsome despair,
the loneliness in his eyes,
the cathedrals I'd entered that night,
and I, wanting only the company of men.
When I left for college that summer,
we never spoke again.
I was told about his death
two weeks after he died.
By then, my memory
of that night had no shadow.
It had grown that thin.

Sycamore

The lake behind our house pulsed like a heart.
I swam in its veins. My shadow draped its rocky shore.
I wore solitude like a bright pair of wings.
        I sketched the anatomy of stars.
Wind taught me to feel.
The ground, what I could contain.
I lived at school, slipped into its silvered hallways
smooth as a fish,
read Rousseau near the water fountain

where I learned about other places to live,
began to see shapes- doors, handles,
how windows divide.
          I learned the symmetry of a lie.
Strange rhythms beat through my body.
Not sure of where I stood on the subject,
I wore mute colors.
I loved the guys in gym class, half-naked, ruddy faced,
everything figured out, scrubbing their hair dry
in the mirrors over the sink.
I watched the towel slide over the ridges of their torsos
that were just becoming, as they dressed, their shoulders
seep through clothes, bodies wet as marble.
Shelves of light funneled through transoms,
opened pockets of steam.
When the bell rang and the other students flew
into the hallways like barn swallows into streams of sunlight,
          I stayed behind until it got dark to study algebra,
and quadratic equations.
What I needed was silence
and a sharp number two pencil.
There was a time I remember how my Father
lifted me to the front yard tree,
carried me on his shoulders
so that I could reach the branches,
pull off the colored leaves in the fall—
the oak, the flamboyant sycamore.
I pasted them in books. They held for years,
the cutout shape of his hands.
Rousseau said a German once wrote an entire book
about a lemon and its dimpled skin,
the fragrance after the inside's
        devoured.

Mitchell Untch

Estate Sale

An oar leans against the side of the Maple tree.
It belonged to the boat we used to own those summers
we spent on the lake waiting for fish,
for the heat to die down, conversation.
Its varnish ripples as if it had just been pulled from the water
having been rescued, as if it were alive.
Not sure how much it's worth: a single oar in a shaft of sunlight.
The sky brims with premature stars.
Shadows drift over the lawn's flat surface.
Neighbors wander in, whisper over tables like refugees.
Warm air blooms from their mouths.
A woman I no longer recognize, picks
through my father's handkerchiefs,
unleashes my mother's scarves, their ghostly bodies of perfume.
Out-of-towners waver. They can't decide between
my Mother's china and a chipped Wedgewood
vase. One girl tries on a hat, shows it to her husband; laughs.
She studies herself in a mirror, rearranges a strand
of violet colored hair, her lipstick, the color of drowned flesh.
The husband points a drill at her as if it were a gun.
An armoire marked down to five dollars
has drawers that skid when you open them, handles that jitter.
When I was growing up my mother hid her cigarettes
in the bottom of the drawer next to her underwear
and silk stockings. I found them one summer, a box
of Lucky Strikes and some matches.
That was the summer my father signed up for the war,
pulled his truck out of the driveway, his toolbox
rattling like an unsteady heart. I remember hearing the gravel rip,
watching the trail of illuminated dust.
I waited under the Maple tree for him to return,
then on the porch until the trees fell silent and the lights
in the upstairs windows grew dark. That night, I sat on my bed
with a flashlight, read Hardy Boys 'til morning.
When my father finally did come back, things were never the same.
Whatever changed had already shown up in my mother's cooking.
Eventually everything sold cheap: the toolbox, the truck,
my mother's pots & pans, my toys, the Ferris wheel, sixteen inches

  tall, flecked
with rust, the blue and red stripes rubbed off where I had imagined
cramming my body into their cold metal seats riding up
with my ticket to wherever the sky would take me.

ERIC HOWARD

To the Terrace House

It was good to see your guts knocked out
enough to fill six truck containers
and a new house rise from your frame
after selling your aluminum sided,
earthquake crooked fugliness.
I regret kicking everyone out of you—
the drunk punk and lame director,
the wannabe P.A. who slept in your shed,
Drummer Girl, a crackhead, a family,
and, finally, me. Your cracks in which
silverfish, ants, and roaches trafficked
are gone like the black widow that charged
out between my eyeballs as I wrenched your drain.
No more crawlies with countless knees
that waved like Misfit mohawks still live in you
to complicate the porn shoot, 500 bucks for your bills,
where I learned the proper rolling of extension cords.
Goodbye, shed that no band played in,
soundproofed too late to get Drummer Girl back.
I am grateful for your coffee pot
and happy pills, work by 8:30, boss says Saturday too,
three million words by Thanksgiving's greasy duck
I cooked for her just once. I respect
your 70s shag carpet that my demented cat
used as a toilet. Thank you, overflowing toilets,
retaining walls that didn't,
and water heater that puked to death
and curled the floor. Goodbye,
Surrealist bathroom and refrigerator,
and Sor Juana Inés de la Cruz,
the hunchback iguana raised on burritos and Diet Sprite.
For your mortgage I taught
English 96 at the local CC, more
students than chairs the first night.
Bless my evaluator's bourbon breath.
I bid goodbye to the neighbor's spite fence.

Eric Howard

Everyone who lived in you—teacher,
mother, faith healer, in-betweener—
picked from the fruit trees of your bolgia.
Goodbye, smoking air conditioner,
unplumb doors and untrue floors,
houseplants dying in galvanized buckets,
and 436 thousand escrow fuckits. I miss
Roger, Sticky Nickki, and Chuckles,
who came to collect from the psycho
Satanist Playboy model, Severina, who was already gone
after getting high in the bathtub. The bullet hole
in your kitchen wall is gone. I washed away
the red paint DIE! with pentacle
from your broken gate. From the chair
on your porch I contemplated
the snow tire, on a wheel, that bounded
through the glass door and thumped twice,
its studs ripping carpet, before going
through a window and down the hill. A burglar
took a boombox through that window after it was fixed.
Goodbye, bedroom that Drummer Girl
didn't come back to till morning
when I left for work and she cranked "Hooker with a Penis."
Ave atque vale, Halloween party I threw
to let her go with, waking up alone on the couch,
door open, various vomits. Goodbye, 300-yard
restraining order circling you and me both.
I'll let go of the 100 drunk attempts to have
that sex again with someone else. Bless
the notches in the shotgun choke
I pressed above my Adam's apple,
brain out of reasons. After a shiver, one—
I'd cause more pain. She said I loved you more than her.
She was love. You were duty. I failed both
and the picture of her in my sweatshirt,
drumming, in the album with mostly empty pages,
by setting it on fire and watching it turn black,
curl cancerous smoke below your grapefruit.
I'll let fall those 50 50-pound bags of gravel
I shouldered down every step to the last level,
when the sun flexed like a drum, like a heart attack.

JUDITH TAYLOR

The Well-Stocked Home

A complacent chair.

The old-fashioned four-poster bed of fate.

You should try to live in a town called Romance or Blue Eyes.

Wallpaper the kitchen with a charming pig and elephant motif.

Only at night are you allowed to open your Pandora's refrigerator.

Keep a large bunch of broccoli on hand to stun any alien being that
    might enter.

If a faucet drips, throw salt over both shoulders, it's faster than
    getting a plumber.

A large green bowl for memories.

A tiny chagrin box for forgetting.

If you're a liar, you'll need a winding staircase

Oldish? Festoon yourself with birdcage earrings and a Stones tee.

A painting of three onions in varying stages of undress and tears.

Your mirror should be silver and a charmer.

A black safe in which to hide your fear of elevators.

A black safe in which to hide your fear of elevator men.

Re: the piano. Teach your children to play toccatas to settle down
    the toucans.

Are the books in your library dialectical, up to a point?

If a marauder enters, throw *Finnegans Wake* at him.

If that doesn't work, try Jonathan Franzen.

One window must be covered with Band-Aids.

For consolation, plant a weeping willow and poisonous mushrooms.

Speak politely to spiders, they produce such complicated jewelry.

A groping and kissing hallway.

A dining room table for oral sex.

If you live near a cornfield, don't ever bake pies.

Edge your house on dark forest, with an occluded path, but known

    to you.

Build a rumba room!

Judith Taylor

How Am I Driving?

Was it because her father taught her to ride a bike
That she'd now need training wheels if she'd ever ride
One, fat chance, and was it because her father taught
Her how to drive that she flunked the driver's test
Three times and it was only she thinks sometimes
Because her lover talked her into buying a used black
Triumph convertible, car that he alone coveted but
Couldn't afford, and because she got sick and tired of him
Driving her and her car to the Rose Garden, to Tilden,
To Mendocino, town she always thought sounded
As if it and everyone in it lied, remembering
Big Daddy growling Mendacity, Mendacity
To Elizabeth Taylor and Paul Newman, that she finally
Went out driving with a man she didn't know well,
Kind despite the hiss of snakes tattooed on his biceps,
Relearned to drive without a man yelling at her
Or grabbing the wheel and took the test and passed
Fine, just fine. It was not because of anyone
That she was, as a child, dyslexic, but it was probably
Because her parents made her become a righty
When she was a lefty (she can tell because when
She throws a ball it's instinctively with the left)
That she still has trouble with directions. On
The other hand (Which one? She's probably confused).
Did her father's rants about Commies, workers
And blacks turn her into a lifelong pinko?
At the end, her dad died diapered and cribbed,
When she thinks of him today the equation of death
And time has subtracted most of her anger, not all,
Certainly, but what's left is transformed into a kind
Of victory: she lives peacefully in a world which he's left.
Now, as she drives up her canyon (over speed limits:
Don't tell the cops) – his little left-wing, left-brain, his
Little bird (not bird-brain), winging right, winging left,
Left on her own, no limits but hers, getting older –
The future's talking back to her (no lie, no lie),
She's flying a narrowing corridor where what's left
Is the certainty that he's the only father she'll ever have
And that she no longer needs one to love or to hate
Or to assign cause to.

Judith Taylor

Black Pot

At dusk, the Blue Ridge sky's laden
with the vague essence of wildness.

For us to sigh blissfully at the sight
of those distant heights, the Romantics

had to arrive hefting their lofty ideas
of the sublime. To some, forests,

those irreplaceable worlds of green
and shadow were "hideous."

Satan and his ilk hung out there. Peasants
said to daughters: Don't go in! Do you want

to be tupped by the devil? OK, don't
answer! Our Salem Witches did Sabbaths

in the woods. The Big Bad Wolf lurks,
the old crone's home of hot sweets squats.

Unless you run fast you will be one sad cookie.
What happens in the forest alters your view

big time of the transparent world. Or
you don't come out. Well, this is old belief.

Now we're cool about the Other denuded
of mystery. What does November taste like?

You say pumpkin, I say smoke. You say
turkey, I say fishes of the air. Not pilgrims,

but the tattered scraps of the Immortals.
Turn the corner of morning, catch the blazing

fox trotting out of the forest. Tumble down
cellar steps, suck out the unaccountable

Judith Taylor

remnants from midnight's larder. Abandon
lanterns, sense the disobedient borders

of the ordinary. Witches with their phallic
broomsticks were the bad girls of yesteryear,

the ones with guts, the untrammeled.
And while we're on the subject, what happened

to a certain witch's wayward nature?
One day she woke, shorn of her wild

turbulent mane. Nearby, mountains ride
the air, stands of ancient oaks remain.

Every thing of the earth's aging, too,
but slowly, slowly. How easy it is now

for her to be tame. It has nothing
to do with goodness.

MARY-ALICE DANIEL

Must Be Some Kind of Spell

A boning knife goes missing.
A guest stole something: the mojo
of the home, disturbed. Your house
isn't haunted—you're just lonely.

Walking through the after-party, you see
chairs arranged in perfect substitution for human congregation:
assembling in groups of two or four, dominating
a space, facing the conversation and food,
policing the exits.

And rings of bottles all around the house.
And sticky ring stains underneath the bottles all over my house—
concentric cones of hospitality
radiating out like crop circles.

They are visual traps. Also, they are sensory traps.
Also, they are fetishes. They are effigies.

Objects are animate. They want to return,
like children or brides, to their owners.

The knife was gone.
The mojo of the house disturbed.
The knife turned up

weeks later, when I bent down to pick up
a dropped mug: it was under my bed, in the middle.

No, you must understand—
it was under the precise center of the bed,

in the spot children hide from their parents' vicious arms,
lined up carefully, pointing perfect and straight
toward the headboard.

Mary-Alice Daniel

Supermoon

The American highway system gives those country towns something to
   do.
All industry as we set out for Nashville. Then green
and green. Greening all over the window—I'm so tired
I'll call that stretch *Boreal*. And we're parched.

A whole airplane part, a wing, dragged
by a truck one lane over. Hurt locomotion. Large
amputation thing. Never had seen anything like it.
It made your day. And then you saw another.

Plus coincidence. Plus disaster. Plus at least 30%

of everything. A small gift of the Earth-Moon-Sun system:
giant moon, big bear of a moon, a frightening
loom. All these things and: the single drop of darkness,
the shadow of an atom. A winning bitch, at last.

Will there be a tornado? God, please make it a fire whirl.

Syzygy (an alignment of three celestial objects)
is a perigee (the point a satellite is closest to a parent body)
and any two related things, alike or opposite.

And if we pass one more clever barn,
I'm done. If we pass one more thing
that looks exactly as it should. If we Big Lie our way out of the South—

We enter the place of dropped bodies: small-town Comerica:
Go for the white skies, bad blood, good food.

MARIANO ZARO

Baldomera

When Baldomera performs her own death
we children sing to her
Baldomera, Baldomera,
se te ve la faltriquera.
Baldomera, Baldomera,
we can see your underwear.

She opens the front doors of the house,
drags an old mattress on the floor,
puts it in the center
with two candles, one on each side.
She dresses in white,
wears a little wreath of paper flowers,
grabs a rosary,
lies on top of the mattress
and waits.

Her face is white.
She is not sick, my mother has told me,
that's just rice powder.

We can see your underwear,
we can see your underwear,
we sing.

We sing until she gets up
and runs and chases us
through the streets.
Sometimes she loses her wreath,
the paper petals fly away.

We are young, she is old,
we run faster, we escape.
One day, one day I will catch you all, she says.

Mariano Zaro

And I know it doesn't matter
how fast I run, how young I am,
one day she will catch me,
like a dog that bites your ankle
and doesn't let go.

Red Swimsuits

We all wear red swimsuits
in this summer camp on the Mediterranean.
It is the rule, the uniform.
That way we are more visible
to the counselors taking care of us.
They are not really counselors,
they are still in college.

We swim on the beach.
It's so hot, the seagulls don't move.
Don't move on top of rocks,
on top of telephone poles.
We go back to the locker room,
we undress, we take a shower.
Today I cannot untie my swimsuit.
I have been in the water until the last minute.
The string is too wet, too tight.
I call one of the counselors.
He is tall,
all adults are tall when you are nine.
He tries the knot,
has big hands,
all adults have big hands.
It is too tight, he says.
He leans over
and unties the string with his teeth.
I feel his stubble against my belly,
for a second. Sandpaper, amber, mint,
danger in the border of flesh and fabric.
Go, hit the shower, he says

Mariano Zaro

I cannot move
I lift my arms between crucifix and butterfly,
I lean against the lockers,
the metal doors rattle.
I see small, soft seagulls coming out of my chest.
Turquoise seagulls, aqua seagulls
that fly fast and hit the ceiling.
They scream, turn, open their beaks,
other seagulls come out of their mouths,
pink seagulls with red eyes,
their wings on my throat,
on my eyelashes.
Finally, they find the narrow window,
they leave the room.

I am alone, the last one there.
From outside, somebody calls my name.
There is salt on the roof of my mouth.

JESSICA GOODHEART

Want

What I want is at the bottom
of a treacherous mine and men

have died in pursuit of it:
fabulous, large and fat

bright as a clock and selfishly glittering.
What I want is mixed in the red

dust of distant planets.
From telescopes in the Mohave

only its brightness can be gleaned.
What I want smells of coffee

and leaves children weeping in the desert.
My own sister limps

through the plaza in her bad shoes
and I do not go to her.

It is that good, that luxurious, spiked as it is
with a liquor made from your tears.

I tried to make do, but what I wanted
required more horsepower than this earth can afford,

a garment made with the silk of a young girl's hair.
I tried to turn away from it, to walk backward,

to reach outward, to crawl on my knees
and ask the grass's forgiveness,

to climb into the ball of myself.
Instead, I toppled governments

with the want of it.
So brightly did it glow, so raucous

Jessica Goodheart

its music, so luminous its pale surface.
I demolished shanty towns

and left a cat in the road, its neck broken
for the glory, the dark, the wonder, the joy.

Let Go

No one ever doubted it was Eve's
mouth on the fruit's white flesh.

Still they watched the security camera tape
over and over, chins perched in judgment,

as though they'd flipped the lid
to their own dark souls.

Friday, words on crisp paper
announced: *To dust they shall return.*

The next week, no one ate anything
grown from seed, no one plucked

anything, not even an eye brow.
Down the long corridors, doors snapped

shut for private conversations
about Eve. We always knew.

There was something about her hands
how they stroked every surface

how they never came to rest.
One of the frames, frozen and tacked

to the message board, revealed a shadow
of a man, not the Adam they remembered,

Jessica Goodheart

the blessed one, always
in the full sunlight of his gleaming teeth.

No, this stranger sucked hungrily
on the sweet, hard end

of what he could not have.

Dear Snow

Fall hard. Blizzard. Blanket
the tracks of the fugitive.

Confuse the dogs.
Let the man run until he cannot.

He has no words for his hurt heart
just hunger and a will of ice.

Let him flee and no one find him.
In summer, he will become

some other thing. Smoke.
Melody of white ash.

Angers that wake us
when we come to know

we won't get more.
This is all there is.

BRUCE WILLIAMS

Arrangement of Optimism

1

God has forgotten my name.
Perhaps only Adam knew it
and Adam and God don't talk
much since the falling
out that covered everything
like snow, colored it like fire.
So maybe God glances at me
with the same muddled ignorance
I use when last year's students
stop me in a restaurant or mall,
or perhaps it's more the way
I look at those grey birds
with the white marks under
each wing, these clumped purple
flowers with their own white
streaks, or the flaked clouds
with scientific labels I should
learn. And He thinks: yes
whatever it is, it's beautiful.

2

Whatever it is, it's beautiful:
learn scientific labels for flaked clouds—
white marks beneath clumped purple.

Bruce Williams

But look at those grey birds
stop in a restaurant or mall

to scatter last year's muddled ignorance
Say, *God glances at me*

the way snow is colored by fire,
which makes a slush of radiance,
smudged quiet everywhere now
that Adam and God
don't talk.

Perhaps only Adam knew it—
God has forgotten my name.

3

Beautiful. Whatever
it is.

God has forgotten my name
like scientific labels for flaked clouds—
Perhaps only
Adam knows

doesn't talk
that's Adam and God
white marks beneath clumped purple,
quiet everywhere.

Bruce Williams

But look at those grey birds
transform slush to radiance,
scatter last year's muddled ignorance
stop in a restaurant or mall.

Say, *God glances at me*
the way snow is colored by fire. . .

PETER J. HARRIS

Genealogy of Nonsense

my trance is the tense you hip me to, love
shepherd of all directions
          aerodynamic lean
& no sex involved
defying gravity like a Maasai boy on his jump into manhood

hipping me, love
          gyroscope along the genealogy of nonsense
unlicensed under my kilt

when I humble myself to you   to you, love
torment shifts to my peripheral vision
undertow of this kinship
mirrored in the fall of a jeweled kufi
ecstasy in my mother's call illuminating dusk
maracas accenting steps to Sunday bathwater
misting the happy ears of well traveled healers
posterity without declaration
is the tense you hipping me to, love

you too?

you too, love?

TIMOTHY GREEN

Poem from Dark Matter

First light through the limbs of the trees. And then
the trees. Each morning the hum of traffic
through the freeway wall. And then the traffic

we're bottled in. Each thing first betrayed
by the shapes around it. As if shadows held
all our weight. Like the empty space that props

each fiery nest of stars, the smooth circumference
of every heavenly body toward which astronomers
might dream. I'm at the kitchen window, early light.

Reading science for tea leaves. Pluto, it seems,
is far colder than we thought. Even the constant
speed of light is decaying. And look where thoughts

can lead: Somewhere in a lonely future, a man
hears his heart stop beating long before the world
goes black. So slow the rate at which nothing

approaches. Or maybe like an ostrich we'll outrun
our past. And then our present. And this, my gift
to you, whatever you'll make of it. The soul, a ship

in a bottle lost at sea. Drops its anchor anyway.

Timothy Green

The Body

in the dream I wake to a poem about trains   what it is that insists

that crawls   clamors   the windowpane clasped shut against a

wind   outside bare branches in a dry heave & I rise   over the

swelling resolution   not to rise   I rise   consider the light

switch   consider the electric blanket warmth   I rise instead

go to the window which is no longer a window but a box full of

moonlight   & down there in the meadow   just a handful of

starspecks in the foxglove   her hair is blue grass   & the first thing

I think of are the wet walls of howe caverns   that tourist trap back

east   the pipe organ   the bridal altar   the river styx

stalactites & stalagmites fusing   the slow settle of limestone

bicarbonate   a blind bat on a billboard unfurling leather wings

unfurling night   unleashing a gust of   supersonic transience

an old dog's call to supper   *twenty miles to go   fifteen   get*

your wallet ready   & there it is again   the unmistakable whistle

the bleating   the bleeding   the letting off of steam   & she's by

the tracks with something in her hands   a silver shining thing &

through the silent distance   through the square hole in my bedroom

wall   I know there's nothing left to call it but hope   though it's just a quarter   a nickel   a dime   general washington's hope

your twenty-five cents worth of hope   a handful of gum balls   a

plastic egg full of costume jewelry that would stain a tiny finger green

it's just the sedimentary   the sentimental dream token hope   the

hope you go to hell   the hope you forgive me   the hope you

remember to hope at least   love   & she sets it down on the far

track as if dropping her hope into the cool slot of a jukebox   the low

clink clambers up from inside my throat   as she steps over   both

tracks   over the shimmering shining thing   over the glittering

fluttering tumbling turning thing now lifting at its edges   the thing

that's always more than whatever it is because   there's the whistle

again   the rumble   a distant thunder   because the past can't

hold the future   the present rumbles on   *five miles almost there*

hush now   it sweeps past   two geometric lines that never touch

& there's the lamplight   the steamstack   the hot metal glow

& at her heels this unnameable sadness   this burden   the eternal

space there between the train's first passing   & the wind that follows

a second later   to wake the body   from its only available dream

ANTONIETA VILLAMIL

Memory of Moss*

I ride the waves of my deprived voice   Swim
in the waters of nowhere   I am an echo
in the memory for the unremembered

The ones that swim
and swim   no island near
no shore   no sand

Perhaps I just imagine that I swim that
I excavate the earth that sustains my flesh
as a promise that enriches old roots

Yes. I dig   I worm into the moist soil
Tender seeds cover my dark garb
austere dirt foots my empty sandals

I dig up with my mortality and scour
into the inner rocks   until the life I am no more
is less than bone in the fugitive soil

Maybe I just pretend that I dig to fly into the wind
and this winding way carries my flesh
a foreshadowing that digs out old voices

Yes. I fly   I swirl into the damp air
Hurricaned dust covers my blue clothes
Warm air cleanses my vacant feet

I dart out with my mortality   and gnaw
into the inner wind until the name I am no more
is less than shards   dashing short-lived clouds

Antonieta Villamil

Perhaps   I just fantasize that I fly   That I am
the burning turmoil that brings forth my flesh
in smoke signals to decode perennial holocausts

Yes. I burn   I am sparks in the bright flames
Ardent soot covers my red rags
Bonfire purifies my unfilled sandals

I shoot out with my mortality and am consumed
into the inner fire   until the person I am no more
is less than ash   in the volatile debris

Maybe I just dream that my voice
whispers in shreds so splinters of their rain
flood the silent waves into which I vanished

I suppose that I appear into this page so
the nightmare unfolds and because I am not
here I am here to bring you the memory of moss

At least   you can dismantle the layers of my skin
Patiently   one by one   so you can heal
the grave embedded in your chest

That grave of which   nobody knows
The grave in your chest with no date
never visited   without an epitaph

Just remember   I am The Disappeared
My name is   And Pedro is my name
even though   it is not I anymore.

*Antonieta's brother Pedro, "died of disappearance" in 1990. He is on the long
list of people that disappear every day in Central and South American Countries.
This poem is a gravestone to his memory.

254

Antonieta Villamil

Syrup of Enchanted Smoke with Green Shoes
to my little brother Pedro

.
Su-
ddenly
you imagine
a pair of green
shoes and you tell
me that I know   what
you want   you want a pair
of green shoes   made of grass
made of leaves   with soles made
of moss and strings made of roots
Quick!   that your legs   want
to be tree   that your arms
are already branches
that a nest is
knitted with
the tip of
your nails
and your
fingers are
writing the
flavors of honey.

MELISSA ROXAS

Geography Lesson

I can show you
the maps
on my body

bruises
the torturers left

these scattered brown things
in a mouth

thick with layers of tongue

sticky keys

and a hung note,

each one
a whole country in itself
dark and beloved

with *Aeta* blood

black pour
red pour
black

dark scabs
on my knees
crack
into a thick brown soup

my nipple
a callous flower

oh

these shiny things
of war

256

Melissa Roxas

> sour breath
> of a dark animal
>
> my brittle bones
> my brittle beast
>
> do not weep

pink callus

Sometimes before
sometimes after
they made me take a bath.

The first time—
with my blindfolds still on,
my hands bound,
one of the soldiers
washed me

My name is Rose
          I am a child of God,
                    she said.

The second time
after I was alone
I tried to cut
using the claw
of a small hair clip
I found hanging on the thin clothes-wire—

but it wasn't sharp enough
it only left
my wrists raw
bumpy red clots
like little grapes about to burst

Melissa Roxas

My body became the most hated
the most beloved
it sat with the grasses of the evening
They banged on the metal door,

                  Out! they said.
There was no more time.

I knew
        They'll make me suffer more
            for trying to die on my own

My body became a flame to open.
There was bone
where there should've been flesh,
I caught the fist landing on my chest,
it danced in the light.

JACKSON WHEELER

Ars Poetica

Because I was sung to as a child. Because my father shot himself when I was ten. Because my mother took in ironing and worked as a janitor. Because my mother would say, she could turn on the radio and I would lie in the crib and listen, quiet as a mouse. Because there was singing on the radio: Kitty Wells, The Louvin Brothers, The Stanley Brothers, The Carter Family, The Stoneman Family; and when I was older, Saturday afternoons with my father's mother, her dark Indian eyes glittering in the twilight of the room – "wrasslen" from Chattanooga, Tennessee, announced by Harry Thornton. Because I watched my uncles slaughter hogs, because I watched my mother kill a chicken for dumplings, because I watched the Rescue Squad drag the Nantahala Lake for drowned vacationers, up from Florida. Because Southern Appalachia was imagined by someone else – I just lived there, in the mountains until I read about it in a book, other than the King James Bible, which is all true my mother said, and says, every jot and St Matthew tittle of it. Because God is a burning bush, a pillar of fire, a night wrestler, a swathe of blood, a small still voice, a whisper in the Virgin's ear. Because my family is full of alcoholics, wife beaters, spendthrifts, and big-hearted people, who give the shirts off their backs. Because their stories lie buried in the graveyards, because their stories have been forgotten, because their stories have been misremembered. Because my father's people said they were from Ireland, down Wexford way. Because my father's father baptized people, because my father's mother bore a child out of wedlock and was part Indian. Because my mother's father got his leg crushed at the quarry, because my mother's mother died of brain cancer in her 50s. My friends think I talk too much, don't talk enough; that I'm too queer for company that I'm not queer enough. My mother's people were Scots and Welsh, three cheers for the beard of Brady Marr, three cheers for the blood on the shields of the Keiths from Wick, three cheers for immigration, the waves of it and the desperation behind it. Let's hear it for King's Mountain and the Scots' revenge for Culloden. Three cheers for extended family, the nameless cousins, all the petty griefs and regrets, the novels never written, the movies never made, the solace of the bottle, the solace of sex, the solace of loneliness of which there is plenty. All hail the poetic arts, and the art of poetry and the knowledge at the heart of it all: *Words bear witness.*

ROBIN COSTE LEWIS

Body in August

Because when I was a child, God would pull me up into Her lap. Because when She pulled me up into Her lap, She would read to me. Because the story She read most was the one I liked least. Because every day She'd open that thin green book and say, This is the story of your life. Because from beginning to end there were only three pages.

I believe in that road that is infinite and black and goes on blindly forever. I believe crocodiles swallow rocks to help them digest crab. Because up until the 20th century, people could still die from sensation. And because my hunger is so deep, I am ashamed to lift my head.

Because memory—not gravity—pins us to this trembling. And when God first laid eyes on us, She went mad from envy. Because if the planet had a back door, we'd all still be there—waiting for the air to approve our entry. Because your eyes were the only time the peonies said yes to me. Because no matter how many times I died, I always woke up again—happy.

Then, last night, after I'd yelled at him for the first time, my new son dreamt we went walking inside the trees. When we came across a squirrel, he said, I'd kicked it. Then the squirrel changed into a thin green book, which we read.

Because when God became a small child, I pulled Her up into my lap. Because when I pulled Her into my lap—to please Her—I'd opened my blouse. Because Her mouth is an impossibly pink place, a gaping raw cathedral, which She opened, teeth-to-nipple, then clamped down.

Robin Coste Lewis

Frame

There'd been a field, a farm, hobos asleep in a chicken coop,
white people whose dogs chased us every day on our way to the pool.
I never knew what, if anything, they grew. Never knew of a harvest.
Never saw a thing begin as seed, or sow its way to plant, flower, fruit.

There was a shack, I remember that, and an old house with an old lady.
She wore a dingy eyelet dress, and paced her porch dry
carrying a shotgun or a broom. Flip-flops, Blow-Pops, Click-Clacks,
Cracker Jacks, we barked Dog Talk with teeth still muddy and black

from Eat the Peg. Soft lime salamanders, fingers a vivid tangerine;
cow hooves grafted to arid grime; date palms with roots so determined
they sucked up all the water from the other things with leaves. We tore
through her property, a whole band of us, day after day, unaware of the
    endings

our bright forms would bring. There wasn't just one, but two
farms, across from each other, and another one, long down
the street, past the pool, next to the Victoria Park Golf Course,
where we never saw one colored man walk into.

Farther out, surrounding us, there were other farms too,
which had been worked, but were not working. There was the pool,
a liquor store, an old house, the golf course, a koi
farm, our new neighborhood, the bakery from Hawaii,

then the landing field for the Goodyear
blimp. You could live here for years and never
understand: were you rural, industrial, or suburban?
We thought we were *home*, but our cardboard

was just slender venture on Negro sprawl.
Before that, it was law: we could not own property
except in certain codes: South Central, Compton, Watts,
where the construction companies were under contract

with the LAPD to tile or tar our addresses onto our roofs,
so when their helicopters needed to shoot,
they'd know—and we'd know too—
who was what and what was who.

Throughout the whole state, every third person
was from Lousy Anna: New Orleans,
Algiers, the West Bank, La Place, Plaquemines
Parish, Slidell, Baton

Rouge. We took pies and cakes to anyone new, but never heard
a sound from the farms. They never brought us nothing either.
No milk, eggs, no butter. It was just clear in the dirt
road we took. Somebody somewhere

was striding in time, but not any of us.
The farmers were lost
and hating it. We were lost
and couldn't care less.

The third farm I remember because I learned to drive in
it, just after they poured the cement, but before they painted the lines.
Shirleen down the street had it, a creamy sea-green 1969
Beetle. My sister was her best friend. Her baby sister was mine.

They were seventeen. We were twelve.
I'd practice in the evening, sitting on the crushed gold
velvet couch in our avocado green shag living
room. I pretended even then—even then—until I could feel it.

My majorette's baton became the stick shift,
cans of butter beans the break, gas, and clutch.
The lesson came early, but I missed it: Ease
up when you let down, let down when you ease up.

Do both at once and you won't ever stall.
Choke that bitch if she don't start –
but choke her
sweetly. I remember when they first broke

the ground. It wasn't bigger than a four-car garage, but we only had
    one car, so what
did we know about how big a library was supposed to be?
It was the biggest any of us had ever seen—the only one
besides the three fragmented shelves

collecting dust in Detention Hall.
We'd hang off of each other, sucking the meat out of a giant
navel orange, tacky with juice and pulp, and watch
the corner of the old farmer's plot open up warm and ripe for us.

Trees felled, bush cleared, ground smooth. Small lathes of wood
the surveyor had joined with white string, stood up straight in the red
    mud
whispering where our books would be. A neutral sky
blue, my first library card, my name in my hand—and typed!—

a first too. The lines of my alphabet so particular, so firm–
my definition now clearer than the Helen-Keller-mirror
in my parents' bathroom
(I liked the *R* most of all).

Then. So that I could see a photograph of an uncommon colored
    body—
besides a burnt body, or a bent body, or a bleeding body, or the
    murdered body
of the Reverend Doctor Martin Luther
King—Junior—

my mother ordered books, the kinds with immature titles
only the seventies could have produced:
Famous Afro-Americans, which had the same amount
of pages as Dr. Seuss.

Our textbooks stuttered over the same four pictures every year: that
    girl
in the foreground, on the balcony: black loafers, white bobby socks,
    black skirt,
cardigan, white collar. Her hand pointing. The others—all men
    looking
so smart, shirt-and-tied, like gentle men on my street, pointing

as well, toward the air—
the blank page, the well-worn hollow space—
from which the answer was always
that same hoary thud.

Every year these four photographs
taught us how English was really a type of trick math:
like the naked Emperor, you could be a King
capable of imagining just one single dream;

or there could be a body, bloody
at your feet—then you could point at the sky;
or you could be a hunched-over cotton-picking shame;
or you could swing from a tree by your neck into the frame.

BRENDAN CONSTANTINE

A Little Black

The children of Juarez have run out
of red crayons. There's so much blood

in their eyes; the bodies of mules
dumped in their schools, hands & heads

by the road, blood in pools, blood
in stories of blood. Before I know it,

I'm planning my own crime, the worst
a poet can commit: to steal suffering,

call it mine. How vivid, I think, what
a strong detail on which to build.

I open my computer, the great self-
making book of our age, search for

more of the story, for the words *run
out of red crayons.* I find children

out of red in Pakistan, in Haiti, no red
left in Afghanistan, none in Georgia.

The children of Sierra Leon have gone
through pink to purple, in Myanmar

they're down to brown. I thought I had
something to add. I have nothing to add

but a little black, the color of the line,
color that consumes all others.

Brendan Constantine

Before the Flood

My father remembers nothing. Or rather
he remembers where it used to be; *See
that building? When I was a kid there was
nothing there. And next door, where
the school is,   nothing.*

We walk through his hometown, down
a street with an Indian name no Indian
lives to translate. *It means Dream River,*
he says, *or Rambling; Confused River
I used to know.*
                    No one believes
their parents were children. That is, you
need more than their word. They have to
do something: stifle laughter, cry into
their hands, stand tiptoe. We all look

younger on tiptoe. My father peers
over a fence, another new building.
This was all sand, he says, *for Bethlehem,
Bethlehem Steel.* His shoe is untied.
He bends to lace it, I almost help. Later

I reach for his hand at a crosswalk.
Let's go back, he says. To how
it was? *No, to the house; I need
to lie down.* We turn and the town
surges under our feet, comes over us

in a wooden tide. I get my arms under his,
kick for both of us. He doesn't try,
doesn't speak when his house goes by.

Brendan Constantine

The last thing I want to do is hurt you

Before that, my love,   long before that,
I'd like to learn another language,   maybe

Portuguese   though people tell me Hindi
& Mandarin are the future,   the tongues

of men on the moon   Which reminds me,
before I hurt you   I want to go to space

& float like   a wing   What do you think
happens to birds in zero gravity; do they panic

or relax,   finally relax   Do they become
fish   Someone must know   by now,

some astro or cosmonaut,   who said,   mostly
to himself,   Don't be afraid,   I just want

to know if you can live   without doing
what you must   The last thing I want to do

is hurt you,   after I see the Grand Canyon,
the pyramids of Giza, the little cave at La Verna

where Saint Francis slept   & listened to God
& went   blind   First   I want to see

Brendan Constantine

my home again,   my heavy home,   the break-
able life   I already know   I want to

have some visions,   too;   angels   or ghosts
or natural disasters   I want to warn the village,

any village,   the dam is breaking,   the fire
is building,   the air is filling with cows   Time

to make a list   How mad will you be
if you don't swim the hundred seas,   don't dive

the sky,   never go   to the cobra show
My love,   you can take it out on me

Brendan Constantine

My Favorite Story Is This One

        where a little blond girl attacks
a family of bears; trashes their home,
eats their food, then runs away
                feeling invaded
My favorite part comes after the end
when the father bear wordlessly repairs
a little chair, a nail held in his black lip,
the mother wipes a table
            with a checkered rag,
& the cub dries his eyes at a window,
watchful ever after
             for a golden anyone

RON KOERTGE

Little, Small, Wee Bear

The rangers may have to shoot the grizzly
who's terrorizing campers down by Tower
Falls. The snuffle in the night, the nose
beneath the flap, the way he maims their
victuals and then mounts the mini-van
looking for a toe-hold in that other world,
the one he strolled in while the porridge cooled.

Pretty soon, though, he is great and huge.
The cottage and the comfy chair are nothing
but a hum that makes him swat his head
until it's gone and he's stopped thinking
about her.   Then the tattered cots remind him
he had a bed and she was in it, hair yellow
as mustard weed. And the rampage begins.

Ron Koertge

Coloring

Here is the handyman with black legs
whistling in spite of gangrene. There
are some smiling cows, red as sores.
A jaundiced mare is chewing peacefully.
Two pea-green farmers chat about nausea.

Cute, but no real grasp of the agricultural
situation. And ending mysteriously
around twelve or thirteen with only
the white crayola intact, used for the silly
sheep, a snowman or the rare Klan meeting.

And no wonder! Whoever heard of The Nobel
Coloring Prize. Who says, "This is my son.
He has a Ph.D. in Coloring." Certainly
no one ever grows up and gets a job
in the Arco Plaza — "The Chairman can't see
you now, he's coloring can't see you now
he's in a crayon seminar can't see you
now he's about to do the barn."

Perhaps some gland does it. Subdued
by greasier hormones it atrophies or sleeps
as we crouch at the window on rainy days
every new hair on our new bodies standing
on end as the pillows become the kids
at school we want to kiss or kill as we
move out of childhood outside the lines
into the real where the sun is not a perfect
cookie in the sky but a big hot thing
like us threatening to destroy the world.

Ron Koertge

Car Wash in Echo Park

Just me, the kid, and random *vatos*
hosing down our precious autos.

A car vac hiccups, coughs and whines.
With hard work, fenders almost shine.

A single boom box emits notes,
and from our unsuspecting throats

the dark blue of a song we know
rises like a u.f.o.

We belt it out. Then almost blush,
lean harder on the worn scrub brush.

I call my kid who says good-bye
to other kids who don't reply.

We drive away, as cool as ice.
She taps my hand. "You guys sang nice."

272

ALICE PERO

Directions for Eating a Mountain

Before eating a mountain,
make sure your face is washed
Dry it with a cloud
Lick the sides, you can drip
molasses on them
Wear something black; it won't stain
The drippings, hot or cold, like a sundae
scare off coyotes' distracting howls
The mountain can be split or sliced, buttered
Some can be whisked into a froth,
but those mountains may not be there at all,
figments, soft, like ripe fruit, melt when you
touch them with a thought
Before biting a mountain, break off a piece,
spiced with a few stray pines
Like sushi, it can be dipped and savored
with green horseradish
Drink the lava before it hardens
But beware, eating a mountain may speed up
your heartbeat, give you strange notions
to climb steep sides, stare at the sky
for centuries, welcome travelers
without speaking
mutely stand against the sun
knowing everything
and nothing

MARY TORREGROSSA

Our Cemetery

has no cypress trees

no sundial, no overgrowth
of forest at its edge

Our cemetery has a chain link fence
a fanciful wrought iron arch
facing a busy street

Darkness does not descend
on this patch of sacred land

we have street lights

There is no chapel, no stained
     glass window, no map
          on a pedestal

you will never lose your way

We are buried on an archipelago
of grass and gravestones

where small American flags
just seem to appear
each Memorial Day

The city grows up around us
a muffler shop, the Diamonte Bar
Hong Kong-style Chinese Food to-go

and still we are laid down

Once in a while a commuter
waiting at the red light notices

a freshly dug hole
and a wreath of flowers

Mary Torregrossa

To Carl

Hey Carl! I saw you today
sitting on the mesh bench
at the Metro station/Gold
Line -red cap or red jacket?
Something red, anyway,
you looked my way into
the train and I waved to
you. Hi! I waved.
"There's Carl!"
I said to Ramon.

Then I got up, moved towards
those cool sliding doors
when Ramon held my elbow,
motioned with his other hand
that we were on the wrong side
of the track and that the door
opened onto the rails from this side.

Imagine! All that with a wave
of his hand - that Ramon! He's
really something! Anyway, Carl
did you see me? I saw you!
Waiting. You turned your head
this way and that, and then
straight ahead, gazing. Oh,
he's thinking, is what I thought.

Do you remember what you
were thinking about? I was
thinking; There's Carlito!

Mary Torregrossa

My train was coming in and
yours was going out, or was it
vice-a-versa? You tell me, Carl,
next time we see each other
somewhere in L A!

JOHN BRANTINGHAM

Icarus Lives

Sure, the wax melted, and he fell,
but his father never came
back to check up on him. Icarus
turned the fall into a dive,
and although he had the wind knocked
out of him, he was able to float
on his back until he was picked up
by a steamer headed to LA.
LA seemed the perfect place for him
at first. He thought he'd capitalize
on his fame, maybe get someone
to ghost write a book for him
and then hit up all the talk shows,
but what he found outside of the hustle
of downtown was a kind of peace
in the suburbs. The weather was nice
in Huntington Beach, and if he let his father
think he was dead, he could avoid any
further hair-brained schemes involving
minotaurs. He unloads real estate now
and has a couple of kids of his own.
The trick, he says in his Hawaiian shirt
at a block party, isn't in telling your kids
not to fly too high, but knowing
when they're old enough for wings.

John Brantingham

A Blessing

In the backyard, the Oldsmobile that hasn't started
in three months has become a table for men.

They pour Cutty Sark over ice in day glo plastic cups
and talk car repair. I'm there too, eight years old

and almost completely deaf, hiding from the sun
under the car and licking my hand for its salt.

Their muffled speech comes to me "ronronron"
as though they're chanting a prayer to Ron,

the god of auto repair. When I'm bored with my hand,
I turn to watch their shuffling feet until their chant

brings me peace, and the salt on my tongue,
the valley heat, the smell of whiskey

and cigarettes, the browning grass beneath me,
and Ron's soothing blessing helps me to drift off to sleep.

John Brantingham

Los Angeles

My love for you, King Smog,
is the love of an old woman
for an old man. I love you with all
of your faults, even sometimes because
of your faults. I love your freeways,
your 5, 405, 605, 105 –
your 10, 210, 110, 710
and for your pesticide beaches
choked with human waste too dangerous
to bathe in but too beautiful
not to. I love you for your LACMA
and MOCA and Getty and your free
jazz concerts and your expensive
jazz concerts. I love you even
when your hills burn orange sherbet,
and when you quake your buildings down,
and when murderous hot winds come
just when I thought the summer heat
was gone. I love you for torrential
rains and mudslides and strip malls
and romances. I love you
when your air creeps in on little
cat claws, climbing onto my chest,
choking me with methane breath.
I love you for your insane Friday
afternoons – everyone on a mission
somewhere and no one moving anywhere.
I love you for Claremont, Santa
Monica, Beverly Hills, Northridge,
and Long Beach, even when
Long Beach Harbor smells
of dirty dish rags three days gone.
And even though I've said
I will leave you, Lord Smog,
the first chance I have, I think
I'll stay with you until they scatter
my ashes on Pacific Coast Highway,
and the desert winds blow me
into the infinity of your endless suburbs.

DOROTHY BARRESI

El Pueblo de Nuestra Señora la Reina de Los Angeles

The brown rats that shimmy
up thatched, hula-skirt palm trees

live closer to the divine,
high in the whispering, razoring fronds.

To them, our glance is a blow.
To scurry their fate.

Half-dissolved in moonlight, released from the ground,
they are astronauts wedged in

capsules of fur and rabies;
they are the true romantics, or else

why would they love so rapaciously
in a paradise unkind?

In all the bungalows below them,
in mansions where the sacred is simple

and the profane complex,
they witness the rhetoric of family: who will shower first,

who folds clothes,
who feels misused.

Who kisses who goodnight, and how.
Dejá everything!

A woman gives herself over to boozy abandonments.
A man lies down with the lamb—

forces himself, actually.
Last week, something precious, a child or a luxury sedan, disappeared

Dorothy Barresi

from a driveway.
The rats know who did it but aren't talking;

no one thinks to ask them.
And we, who choose to believe ourselves

fundamentally ratless,
hump and snout and the scaled reptilian tail trembling,

mean no harm,
though harm will be done.

Dorothy Barresi

Security

Los Angeles International Airport, November, 2001

Each checkpoint
was different.

At one we were asked
to recite
The Lord's Prayer.

At another,
to sip from the wheezing guard's
cold coffee mug.

Are you a wolf?
Have you ever been a wolf?

Pancakes were fried
in a gentleman's hat
who wished only to visit his mother

in flat Cincinnati.

A rooster was decapitated
and his head thereafter
reaffixed;
though we knew not how,

it felt like love
to be considered so carefully.

The woman behind me
began to cry—
was there a little leak in her fate?

It was the world and the next day.

It was the apprehension of things unseen:

Dorothy Barresi

would, for example,
the sky accept
our names today?
The crossed blue circuitry
of the sky?

A pipe-and-curtain stanchion
was erected
around a toddler
who'd made a verbal error.

Outside, whipped cream was being pumped
along the runways—
"emergency foam,"
we supposed,

though no one ever landed
or took off.

A stewardess with a nosebleed
ran past,
chased by her suitcase.

Dorothy Barresi

Poem to Some of My Recent Purchases

Durable goods,
sweet and crude,
I calculate your worth
by the glory available,
divide by dollars spent, my relief,
the exact nature and angle of my pleasure: *abide with me*, things say.

We won't leave you here alone.

Lipstick, pantyhose (Donna Karan), A-line cashmere skirt,
mid-heel spectator pumps, and lately,
a high amp juice extractor
for vegetables and fruit—

I choose you
because each day for 662 years my grandparents ate
bologna sandwiches, and then
Hoover came in
and things got really bad.
900 years of onions and reflex courage.
5,648 years of ward bosses, head busters, union dues, babies,
Fiorella La Guardia leading the National Anthem
at Yankee Stadium, and no
roses or raises, ever.

Responsibility: my dad's dead dog
when he was growing up, schlepping *Boys' Life* door to door.

Dog-tired: my second cousin on my mother's side.

Makeshift Gratitude: my mother on cold school mornings
slapping mustard around
in her bathrobe, cigarette atilt in her lips.
She made the bologna sandwiches
I was destined to unwrap.

Bracelet, earrings, tanzanite toe ring
(I liked peridot better
but they didn't have my size),

Dorothy Barresi

if I never buy anything,
how will I distract myself?
How will I weigh myself down
when the last winds come to find me unworthy with

wailing, gnashing, and proclaiming
by which I am sucked up and
bare as a soup bone in butcher paper
thrown free?

The big wars are over
but the small ones never end.
What shall I save?

In my personal bedroom community the babies are not always
        kissed or fed;
boys murder boys;
politicians dance with underage girls named
Absolute Value or Agnes Dei
while buses loaded with dead pensioners
leave on the hour
for Indian gaming in Palm Springs. What I am saying,

my dear, dear purchases,
is that I refuse to be chronically wistful.
I tear open your clear wrappings with my teeth
in the front seat of my car.

I love you.

And if not you, precisely,
I adore the moment the salesgirl hands you over
as if proffering
the sunset and all its glowing fruits.
Jesus is my homeboy, her lovely tattoo tells me,
and my son with be safe
if I will only pray.

Dorothy Barresi

Bracelet, lampshade, purse, perfume
(Coco, by Chanel),
lemongrass votive candles
too pretty to burn,
am I to understand
my sarcasm
will not help me?

In the ascendant American paradigm,
I leave Macy's with an armload of usable truth
in a world of plenty.
The sparrows do not line up
in their sniper nests against me,
my credit rating holds,

I buy,
not to escape the world
but to draw it nearer. To build
more world up around me.

Bracelet, perfume, lampshade, purse,
jewel-horde, dream-horde,
cast your spell. Consume me as you do.
Take me home,
where I might hold you in my lap a while,
now that I am often afraid.

ELOISE KLEIN HEALY

Dark

I'll tell you why I'm afraid of the dark.
It has its own idea.
It's like a bullet.
It doesn't want to know what you know.

The dark is under.
It fits a place to put a hand but I can't see.
It's like a voice behind a door.
It can be just about anything I want to hear.

Darkness comes in every size of threat:
the dark cocoon at the end of my life,
storms that turn the sky into an empty can of dark
fitting snug onto the horizon,
the dark in putting my head in hands,
my head into the cave of a person I don't love anymore.

I'll tell you again why I'm afraid of the dark.
I can see it coming
and can't ever tell just when it has arrived.
I sense it thin and waiting between the pages of books
but it's too fast even for a good reader.

From that place darkness
comes a phone call erratic with grief.
It fills the story called "dying in your sleep"
and was the only time left for voodoo to take,
for rapists to dress in.

I can't get a grip on darkness
though it wears my imagination like a shroud.
I've started hearing sunsets as cracking twigs.
I've taken to hiding a piece of flint in my shoe.

Eloise Klein Healy

My Love Wants to Park

My love wants to park
in front of your house.

Thank God.
It's been driving me crazy
going around and around the block.

It's started breaking laws,
obsessively rolls through boulevard stops,
changes lanes without looking back.

It's taken over the transmission,
drops into second when I try to drive by
and rolls down its own windows.
I had to pull the horn wires
after it learned to "a-uugah"
at the sight of your address.

So just come out here please.
Please, just look under the hood
and kick the tires.

Try to stay away from the back seat.

Eloise Klein Healy

Artemis in Echo Park

I turn out the driveway, point down the street,
bend where the road bends and tip down the hill.
This is a trail even under asphalt.
Every street downtown cuts through adobe
and the concrete wears like the curve
of a bowl baking on a patio or the sway of a brick wall
drying in the sun.
The life before cement is ghosting up
through roadways that hooves and water
have worn into existence forever.
Out to Pasadena, the freeway still behaves
like a ravine, snaking through little valleys.
The newer roads exist in air, drifting skyward,
lifting off the landscape like dreams of the future.
We've named these roads for where they end—
Harbor Freeway, Ventura Freeway, Hollywood Freeway—
but now they all end in the sky.

ROBERT MEZEY

A Glimpse of Beau Jack

Philadelphia, 1946.
Night. My father and I are walking home
along a pavement raked by swirling snowflakes
wherever the wind kicks up. Having just emerged
from under the beamed shadows of the El
we cross to the Arena, heading home
– to mashed potatoes, sisters, downcast eyes,
anger and sullen silence – past the wall
in which a door stands open and I see
in luminous blackness hundreds of black shapes,
heads and shoulders, the sides of faces silvered
in swirls of smoke, the embers of cigars
glowing an instant and then blacking out –
far off in the black depths the source of light,
the canvas square of ring circled by kliegs
and a slim brown man who has a bigger man
pinned on the ropes, digging blood-red gloves
methodically, like a man chopping wood,
into his ribs, the white skin splotching pink.
Could I have seen at that distance the rocking
and ripple of muscle under the bronze skin
or did I just imagine all of this?
It couldn't have been much more than a second –
my father was a very impatient man –
but there it is, as radiant as just now.
My arm was jerked hard, I was dragged away
wondering desperately who the man was – then
there he was on a poster, fists cocked, poised,
smiling behind his gloves. I have forgotten
the name of his opponent but not his name.
I loved him, and I wanted what he had –
not the jeweled belt, the title, money, fame –
what could they mean to an eleven-year-old?
No, what I wanted was the pride and power,
prowess and speed and grace, and even more,
fearlessness in the face of bigger men.
And that most beautiful of names – Beau Jack.

Robert Mezey

Hardy

Thrown away at birth, he was recovered,
Plucked from the swaddling-shroud, and chafed and slapped,
The crone implacable. At last he shivered,
Drew the first breath, and howled, and lay there, trapped
In a world from which there is but one escape
And that forestalled now almost ninety years.
In such a scene as he himself might shape,
The maker of a thousand songs appears.

From this it follows, all the ironies
Life plays on one whose fate it is to follow
The way of things, the suffering one sees,
The many cups of bitterness he must swallow
Before he is permitted to be gone
Where he was headed in that early dawn.

There

It is deep summer. Far out
at sea, the young squalls darken
and roll, plunging northward,
threatening everything. I see
the Pacific moving in slow
contemplative fury
against the rocks, the beaten
headlands, and the towns sunk deep
in a blind northern light. Here,
far inland, in the mountains
of Mexico, it is raining
hard, battering the soft mouths
of flowers. I am sullen, dumb,
ungovernable. I taste myself
and I taste those winds, uprisings
of salt and ice, of great trees
brought down, of houses and cries
lost in the storm; and what breaks
on that black shore breaks in me.

WILLIAM ARCHILA

Guayaberas

In my boyhood, all the men

wore them, a light body shirt
with pleats running down the breast,
two top pockets for pens, notepads,

two bottom ones for keys or loose change,
each sewn with a button

in the middle of the pouch,
a complement tailored to the slit
at the side of the hip. If you look

at photographs in family albums,
men stand against palm trees,

their short-sleeved guayaberas
caught in sunlight, their Panama hats
tipped to the sky. There's a black and white

of my father, stumbling along fields
of cane, head full of rum,

mouth in an o, probably
singing a bolero of Old San Juan.
On days like these, the sun burned

like an onion in oil. Women hung
guayaberas on windows to dry.

Shirtless, men picked up their barefoot babies
off the floor, held them against their bellies
as if talking to a god. Even my school uniform

was a blue guayabera, but nothing
like my father's favorite: white,
long-sleeved, above the left breast

William Archila

a tiny pocket, perfectly slender for a cigar,
arabesque designs vertically stretched.

When the evening breeze lulled
from tree to tree, he serenaded

my mother, guitars and tongues of rum
below her balcony; the trio strumming,
plucking till one in the morning.

I don't know what came first,
war or years of exile,
but everyone — shakers of maracas, cutters

of cane, rollers of tobacco — stopped wearing them,
hung them back in the closet, waiting

for their children to grow,
an arc of parrots to fly across the sky
at five in the evening. In another country,

fathers in their silver hair sit
on their porches, their sons, now men,

hold babies in the air, guayaberas nicely pressed.

William Archila

Bury This Pig

Behind the cornfield, we scaled the mountainside
        looking for a foothold among the crags,

rooting out weeds, trampling on trash,
        the trek as if it were a holy crusade:

bodies armored, mounted on horses,
        banners fluttering in the air.

Then one morning, we stumbled upon the thing,
        dead, cramped in a ditch, covered in ants,

trotters grimy, a purple snout of flies
        and not a dollop of blood,

but a thick piece of hide, cradling
        about fifty pounds of hog.

Someone said, "Kush! Kush!"
        as if to awaken the thing.

I thought about the carcass, blood-slick,
        staggering into the room,

grumbling and drowning as if deep in the mud,
        eyes buckled in fear,

bones breaking down to the ground, open
        to the chop and tear of human hands:

pork and lard, forefeet, fatback cut into slabs,
        an organ fattened and butchered.

It continued for weeks, a few of us
        meeting in the afternoons

just to look at the steaming belly, maggots
        stealing the gray of the brain,

each time, one more barefoot boy
        probing the eye socket with a stick.

William Archila

Some of us came back armed
        with picks and bars, shovels dusty in our hands,

until the ground groaned with war.
        The sky fell and cracked the earth.

How was I to know
        they would be hooked, hacked,

snouts smashed on the wall,
        their bodies corkscrews on the floor?

How was I to know
        I would bury this pig, rock after rock?

William Archila

Radio

"Puedo escribir los versos más tristes esta noche.
Escribir, por ejemplo, 'La noche está estrellada....'"

That was Neruda through a small plastic portable,
blue with white knobs, when I was ten
and mother woke me to listen

by the red needle of the dial, its window
throwing a half-yellow light in the bedroom,

his voice reaching the darkest corner
of the house, words full of rain, ancient,

from a foreign planet, lapping at my bedside,
fat waves rocking against a boat, prow

reaping through the waters, a sound
like the whoosh of pine trees bending.

The set was big enough for the rusted gun
mother hid inside, right above the batteries,

a piece ready to target soldiers
on rooftops, camouflaging the dawn,

or the men of tattered clothes, tired eyes,
rifles in their hands, running down
coffee mountain to palace wall.

The poems kept coming, calmed,
relaxed, as if walking back
from a lake, the rise and fall

of waves closing over each other,
ignorant of my father on the phone,
calling long distance from Los Angeles,

William Archila

his voice, a buzz and a click, clipped
by the blackouts of a tiny country.

Who knows what kept
my father in the north? Perhaps
it was the city lights of a woman,

long snouts of avenues
clutching their tongues, unrolling
the drunken dollar flat on his hand.

Perhaps it was the vertebrae of broken bodies
caught in the gutter. Who knows

if he knew that wind flew
around our house, howling like a dog?

That his wife came to bed
as if rejected by the moon once again,

radio in the crook of her arm
tuned to the dark shade of pines,
"lento juego de luces, campana solitaria."

I lay in bed, my mother's breath lost
deep in the absence of her husband – my ears
wide open to darkness,

listening to the lines of a faint voice
crackle and glow, a radio that enters evening
like a boatman standing in the mist,

feeling waves roll underneath, pulling me
through the slow nights of a small war.

William Archila

This is for Henry

It always starts here,
over the chain-linked fence
          with crooked fingers,

leather shoes, running
across the railroad tracks,

          no sound but a gasp
for breath, our white shirts flapping
like flags, cops in black behind.

Sometimes, it's you kneeling
at the corner of the liquor store, handcuffed,
          baton blow
to your back, flopping
to the ground, a grunt
          of flesh and bone,
your golden tooth shining.

This is what I remember
when I drive through east L.A., the boys leaning
          against the wall, rising above trash
                    cans, beer bottles,

baggy pants and black
shades, long white shirts
          with two clown faces
above the left breast: one laughing,
          the other crying.

          I think
we were fifteen
when we worked in the dark kitchen,
                    restaurant heat
                    of vegetables and spices,
bags of rice, boxed beer from China.

William Archila

During breaks, you stood in the alley,
        your shirt over the shoulder
like a towel, whistling
at the girls strolling

their short skirts, exposing
        the lighter skin
            of their bodies.

Around midnight, after carrying
        the last crate of dishes, we untied
our wet aprons.

                I sat across from you
munching on bread, Italian sausages,
swigging on a bottle of wine,
your talk thick as honey -
                marijuana visions of North
                America: blonde girls and their bikinis,
                low riders at night, you in a zoot suit
                        and Bruce Lee.

Fifteen years will pass
before I think of you again,
deportation to a village
        between cane fields at dusk,

        your disappearance between the Eucharist
        and the clang of the bell
            early Sunday morning.

I'm a teacher now,
fingers of chalk, papers piled around me.
        Sometimes, in the dark eyes
        of students, you appear,
                your white shirt, shiny shoes,

                your back slouched
                at the board, cracking the English grammar.

William Archila

On the street corner, a boy
flashes a hand sign

and it all starts again,
climbing over the fence, running through east L.A.

Biographies & Acknowledgements*

Linda J. Albertano represented Los Angeles at the One World Poetry Festival in Amsterdam. For the L.A. Theatre Center, she was commissioned to create a full-length experimental work. With Anne Waldman and others, she read in Allen Ginsberg's Memorial at the Wadsworth Theater, and she's featured on the Venice Poetry Wall with noted poets such as Wanda Coleman and Charles Bukowski. She is a member of the trio Nearly Fatal Women.

"Beloved" has been published in the Los Angeles Institute of Contemporary Arts Journal and was selected for the NELA public arts project, "Poetry in the Windows."

William Archila is the author of *The Art of Exile*, which won an International Latino Book Award in 2010. He was awarded an Emerging Writer Fellowship by The Writer's Center in Bethesda, MD. William holds an MFA from University of Oregon and currently lives in Tujunga, California with his wife, the poet Lory Bedikian. His second book *The Gravedigger's Archaeology* recently won the Letras Latinas/Red Hen Poetry Prize (March, 2015).

"Radio," "Guayaberas," "Bury This Pig," and "This is for Henry" are from *The Art of Exile (*Bilingual Press, 2009). AGNI previously published "Bury This Pig." Hanging Loose Press previously published "Guayaberas", and "Radio" was published in Portland Review. North American Review previously published "This is for Henry."

Mary Armstrong is a native of Los Angeles, where she serves as the financial officer of the Los Angeles Poetry Festival. Her poems have appeared in over 30 literary journals, including The Missouri Review, Nimrod, Burnside Review, Potomac Review, and the anthologies *Grand Passion* and *Open Windows: Selections from Poetry in the Windows Winners 1995 - 2003*. In 2013, her chapbook, *Burn Pit,* won the Slapering Hol Press Chapbook Competition.

"The Shape of Light" was previously published in Nimrod International Journal Chapbook and *Burn Pit.*

RD Armstrong got serious about poetry in 1993. He has 18 chapbooks, 10 books, so far. He has been published in over 300 poetry magazines, anthologies, blogs and e-zines. He started the Lummox Press in 1994; after 20 years & a few hundred titles, it's still one of the best kept secrets in L.A.

"Corazon" was published online at Metropolis (France) in 2008.

"Corazon" and "While Reading Lorca" are from his book *Fire and Rain, Selected Poems 1993 - 2007* (Lummox Press, 2008).

Erika Ayón emigrated from Mexico when she was five. She grew up in South Central, Los Angeles, and received her BA in English from UCLA. She was selected as a 2009 PEN Emerging Voices Fellow and was also chosen by The Los Angeles Poetry Festival to read in Newer Poets XV as part of the ALOUD Series at The Los Angeles Central Library. Her work has appeared in The Accentos Review,*Strange Cargo*, an Emerging Voices Anthology, and will be in the anthology *Orangelandia*.

"Love Letter to Octavio" first appeared in KCET'S Departures Series; "Thirteenth Child" was published in a broadside for Poetry Super Highway's Reading Series. A version of "Apá's Eden" was included in the Frying Pan News feature, "Five Poems the Next Mayor Should Read."

Tony Barnstone, the Albert Upton Professor of English at Whittier College, has published 18 books, a poetry chapbook, and a music CD. His poetry books include: *Pulp Sonnets*; *Beast in the Apartment*; *Tongue of War: From Pearl Harbor to Nagasaki*; *The Golem of Los Angeles*; *Sad Jazz: Sonnets*; and *Impure: Poems by Tony Barnstone* .

"The 167th Psalm of Elvis", "The California Book of the Dead" and "Azusa Boulevard" are all from *The Golem of Los Angeles* (Red Hen Press, 2008). "Commandments" is from *Impure: Poetry by Tony Barnstone* (University Press of Florida, 1999).

Dorothy Barresi is the author of four books of poetry: *American Fanatics* (University of Pittsburgh Press, 2010); *Rouge Pulp*; *The Post-Rapture Diner*, winner of an American Book Award; and *All of the Above*, winner of the Barnard College New Women Poet's Prize. She has received Fellowships from the National Endowment for the Arts and the North Carolina Arts council. She is Professor of English and Creative Writing at California State University, Northridge, and lives in Los Angeles with her husband and sons.

"Security" appeared in *American Fanatics* (University of Pittsburgh Press, 2010). "Poem to Some of My Recent Purchases"; "El Pueblo de Nuestra Senora la Reina de Los Angeles" in *Rouge Pulp* (University of Pittsburgh Press, 2002). "Poem to Some of My Recent Purchases" won a Pushcart Prize and was reprinted in *Pushcart Prize XXVIII: Best of the Small Presses* (Pushcart Press, 2004).

Lory Bedikian's *The Book of Lamenting* was awarded the 2010 Philip Levine Prize for Poetry. She earned her MFA in Poetry from the University of Oregon. Her manuscript was selected several times as a finalist in the Crab Orchard Series Competitions. Lory has received a grant from the Money for Women/Barbara Deming Memorial fund.

Poems included here were published in *The Book of Lamenting* (Anhinga Press). "The Mechanic" was previously published in Grist.

Molly Bendall is the author of four collections of poetry, *After Estrangement, Dark Summer, Ariadne's Island* and most recently, *Under the Quick* from Parlor Press. She has also co-authored with the poet Gail Wronsky *Bling & Fringe* from What Books. Her poems have appeared in the anthology *American Hybrid: The Norton Anthology of the New Poem*. Molly teaches at the University of Southern California.

"Pitch This" was previously published in *Ariadne's Island* (Miami University Press, Oxford, Ohio, 2002) and prior to that The American Poetry Review.

Michelle Bitting holds an MFA in Poetry from Pacific University, OR, and is pursuing a PhD in Mythological Studies at Pacifica Graduate Institute. She's had poems in APR, Prairie Schooner, Narrative, diode, the L.A. Weekly, Manor House Quarterly, and an essay in *The Enchanting Literary Verses*. Her book *Good Friday Kiss* won the DeNovo First Book Award and *Notes to the Beloved*, won the Sacramento Poetry Center Award. Michelle has taught in the UCLA Extension Writer's Program, and at Twin Towers prison with a grant from Poets & Writers Magazine.

"Black Guitar" was previously published on Linebreak & Verse Daily. "Morning, Highway 126" was published in The American Poetry Review.

Laurel Ann Bogen is the author of ten books of poetry and short fiction. Since 1990 she has been an instructor in the Writers' Program at UCLA Extension where she received the Outstanding Instructor of the Year Award in 2008. In 2016, Red Hen Press will publish *All of the Above: New and Selected Poems, 1975-2015.* She is a founding member of the performance trio Nearly Fatal Women, which broke (or tied) attendance records for Beyond Baroque Literary Arts Center in 2014.

The three poems featured here first appeared in *Washing a Language* (Red Hen Press, 2004).

John Brantingham's work has been featured on Garrison Keillor's "Writer's Almanac," and he has had hundreds of poems in magazines in the United States and England. His newest poetry collection, *The Green of Sunset,* is from Moon Tide Press. He is the writer-in-residence at the dA Center for the Arts and directs the San Gabriel Valley Poetry Festival. He teaches at Mount San Antonio College.

303

Poems reprinted here come from his collection *East of Los Angeles* (Anaphora Press). "Los Angeles" was also published in Freefall Magazine. "A Blessing" also appeared in ASKEW.

Elena Karina Byrne is an editor, Poetry Consultant / Moderator for The Los Angeles Times Festival of Books, Contributing Editor for the Los Angeles Review of Books, and Literary Programs Director for The Ruskin Art Club. She is the former Regional Director of the Poetry Society of America. Publications include a Pushcart Prize, Best American Poetry, Yale Review, Paris Review, Verse & APR. Books include: *The Flammable Bird, MASQUE* and the forthcoming *Squander* and *Voyeur Hour: Meditations on Poetry, Art and Desire.*

"Moon Mask" was published in Yale Review. Varuna, in Hindu mythology, shines at night and is linked with the moon.
"Vertigo Mask" was published in *Valley of Contemporary Poets Anthology.*

Luís Campos is a native of the Dominican Republic. He was a member of the original Venice Poetry Workshop, which began in 1969. He received first prize in the Bay Area Poets Coalition Contest, 1983, for "Shooting on W. 92nd St." He was the recipient of the Unknown Reader Award sponsored by Electrum Magazine, 1984, for "Electric Poem in AC Minor" His poetry has appeared in The Los Angeles Times, Venice 13, Bachy 1, *An Anthology of Environmental Poetry* and other publications.

"At the Hospital" was published in Caffeine, 1995, and again in the online magazine, Cultural Weekly, May 2014.

Hélène Cardona is the author of *Dreaming My Animal Selves* (Salmon Poetry), winner of the Pinnacle Book Award and the 2014 Readers' Favorite Award in Poetry; *The Astonished Universe* (Red Hen Press, 2006); and *Life in Suspension*, forthcoming from Salmon Poetry in 2016. *Ce que nous portons* (Éditions du Cygne), her translation of *What We Carry* by Dorianne Laux, came out in September 2014. She also translated *Beyond Elsewhere* by Gabriel Arnou-Laujeac. Hélène holds a Master's in American Literature from the Sorbonne.

"Notes From Last Night" was previously published in *Dreaming My Animal Selves* (Salmon Poetry, 2013)

Wanda Coleman (1946-2013) grew up in the Watts neighborhood of Los Angeles. Her poetry collection *Bathwater Wine* (Black Sparrow Press, 1998), received the 1999 Lenore Marshall Poetry Prize. A former medical secretary, magazine editor, journalist, and Emmy-winning scriptwriter, Coleman received fellowships from the National Endowment for the Arts and the Guggenheim Foundation. Her books of poetry include

304

Mercurochrome: New Poems (2001), which was a finalist for the National Book Award in poetry.

"I Live for My Car" is from *Imagoes* (Black Sparrow, 1983); "Wanda Why Aren't You Dead" is from *Heavy Daughter Blues* (Black Sparrow, 1987); "Neruda" *Hand Dance* (Black Sparrow, 1992) and "Sonnet for Austin" are from *The Love Project* (Red Hen Press, 2014)

Larry Colker is the author of *Amnesia and Wings* (Tebot Bach, 2013), and *What the Lizard Knows* (chapbook, 2003). Larry has co-hosted the Redondo Poets weekly reading at Coffee Cartel in Redondo Beach, CA, for 15 years. Poets & Writers, Inc., selected his entry as the 2007 poetry winner of the California Writers Exchange Contest.

"The Leap" was originally published in The Sun, and "Projector" first appeared in The Cortland Review.

Brendan Constantine has had poems in FIELD, Ploughshares, Zyzzyva, Ninth Letter, Poetry Daily, ArtLife, and Hotel Amerika, and his books include *Birthday Girl with Possum* (Write Bloody, 2011) and *Calamity Joe* (Red Hen Press, 2012). He has received grants and commissions from the Getty Museum, James Irvine Foundation, and the National Endowment for the Arts. A popular performer, Brendan has presented his work throughout the U.S. and Europe, and appeared on NPR's "All Things Considered."

"Before the Flood" first appeared in the journal Redivider and in the book *Calamity Joe* (Red Hen, 2012) along with "My Favorite Story Is This One." "A Little Black" appears in *Birthday Girl with Possum* (Write Bloody, 2011). "The last thing I want to do is hurt you" first appeared in the journal Ghost Town.

Mary-Alice Daniel was born in Nigeria and raised in England and Nashville, Tennessee, but has adopted Los Angeles as her home. Her work has appeared or is forthcoming in New England Review, Mid-American Review, PANK, New Orleans Review, and Hayden's Ferry Review. She is currently an Annenberg Fellow in USC's PhD Program in Creative Writing.

"Must Be Some Kind of Spell" was originally published in Anti-. "Supermoon" was originally published in Word Riot.

Carol V. Davis is the author of *Between Storms*. She won the 2007 T.S. Eliot Prize for *Into the Arms of Pushkin: Poems of St. Petersburg*. Twice a Fulbright scholar in Russia, her poetry has been read on NPR, Radio Russia and at the Library of Congress. She teaches at Santa Monica

College, Antioch University, L.A. and is poetry editor of the *Los Angeles Jewish Journal*.

"Marshland" was originally published in Ploughshares (vol. 36, no. 1, Spring 2010) and in *Between Storms* (Truman State University Press, 2012).

Marsha de la O's book *Black Hope* won the New Issues Poetry Prize from the University of Western Michigan and an Editor's Choice Award. Her work has been anthologized in *Intimate Nature: The Bond Between Women and Animals* (Ballantine), *Bear Flag Republic: Prose Poems and Poetics from California* (Greenhouse Review Press), and the poetry workshop handbook *One for the Money: The Sentence as Poetic Form* (Lynx House Press).

"Chinese Lantern" was published in the online journal, Chaparral in 2012. "Janet Leigh is Afraid of Jazz" and "Blue Parrots" were included in *Black Hope*.

Linda Dove has published two award-winning collections of poetry, *In Defense of Objects* (Bear Star, 2009) and the chapbook *O Dear Deer*, (Squall, 2011). She holds a Ph.D. in Renaissance literature and was a college English professor for many years. She currently lives in Monrovia, California.

"St. Nicholas of Tolentino Confronts His Moral Ambivalence in the Buffet Line" was previously published by Moonday Poetry Online.

Kim Dower was born in New York City and has lived in Los Angeles for over 30 years. Her poetry has appeared in "The Writer's Almanac," Ploughshares, Rattle, Barrow Street, The Los Angeles Review. Two collections of her work, *Air Kissing on Mars (2010)* and *Slice of Moon* (2013), were published by Red Hen Press.

"Boob Job" first appeared in Rattle #40, Summer, 2013, and then in *Slice of Moon* (Red Hen Press, 2013). "Extraction" was also in *Slice of Moon*.

Jawanza Dumisani is a native Detroiter whose first full-length collection is *Black Raising Cane Over Red* (Glover Lane Press, 2014). Since joining The World Stage Anassi Writer's in 1997, he earned a scholarship in '03 and studied with Suzanne Lummis at the UCLA Extension Writers' Program. In '05 he received THE PEN AWARD. He served as Director of Literary Programming at The World Stage from 2005 to 2011. He serves as Executive Director of Lady Between The Lines Art Agency.

"Odell's Desire" and "Daddy's Epitaph" both appear in *Black Raising Cane Over Red.*

Yvonne M. Estrada is a poet and photographer. Her recent chapbook, *My Name On Top of Yours,* pairs sonnets about and original photographs of graffiti. Her poetry has been published in San Gabriel Valley Quarterly, Catena, Mischief, Caprice & Other Poetic Strategies, Pulse Magazine, GuerrillaReads.com, #8, Verse Wisconsin, and the *2011 Poem of the Month Calendar.*

"Johnny Doe" was previously published in Pulse Magazine; "A Fresh Coat of Night" appeared in *My Name on Top of Yours,* (Silverton Books, Los Angeles. 2013); "String Theory No Joke" was published on the UCLA Live website.

Jenny Factor's *Unraveling at the Name* (Copper Canyon Press), was a finalist for the Lambda Literary Award. She's had poems in the Paris Review, Prairie Schooner, Nerve.com, and anthologies such as *The Best American Erotic Poems* (Scribner, 2008). She received her BA from Harvard College and MFA from the Bennington Writing Seminars. She serves as Core Faculty at Antioch University Los Angeles, the nation's first low-residency MFA program devoted to literature and social justice.

"The Street Hawkers" was originally published in Prairie Schooner (Spring, 2010), and was reprinted in Work, an online collaboration between Prairie Schooner and the Cordite Review.

B.H. Fairchild is the author of seven books of poetry, the most recent of which is *The Blue Buick: New and Selected Poems* (W.W. Norton, 2014). He is the recipient of NEA, Guggenheim, and Rockefeller (Bellagio) fellowships and several awards, including the National Book Critics Circle Award, the Kingsley Tufts Award, The William Carlos Williams Award, and Pushcart Prizes in both poetry and the essay.

"Rave On" and "A Starlit Night" are from *Early Occult Memory Systems of the Lower Midwest* (W.W. Norton, 2003). "The Invisible Man" is from *The Art of the Lathe* (Farmington, Maine: Alice James Books, 1998).

Alexis Rhone Fancher has had work in Rattle, The MacGuffin, Slipstream, The Mas Tequila Review, Poeticdiversity, Fjords Review, and H_NGM_N. Her latest collection is *How I Lost My Virginity to Michael Cohen and Other Heart Stab Poems* (Sybaritic Press, 2014). In 2013 she was nominated for two Pushcart Prizes. Alexis is poetry editor of the on-line magazine of art, politics and culture, Cultural Weekly.

"The Seven Stages of Love" is published in *How I Lost My Virginity To Michael Cohen and Other Heart Stab Poems* (Sybaritic Press, 2014).

Jamie Asaye FitzGerald's poetry has appeared the journals Works & Days, Mom Egg Review, Cultural Weekly and Literary Mama. She received an Academy of American Poets College Prize at the University of Southern California and an MFA in poetry from San Diego State University. She lives in Los Angeles with her husband and daughter, and works for Poets & Writers.

Mary Fitzpatrick's poems have been finalists for the Joy Harjo Poetry Prize and the Inkwell Poetry Contest; featured in Mississippi Review, Atlanta Review and North American Review as contest finalists; and have also been published in Agenda, Albatross, The Dos Passos Review, ASKEW, The Georgetown Review, Writers at Work and in anthologies *Beyond the Lyric Moment*, *A Bird Black as the Sun,* and Cancer Poetry Project 2. A graduate of UC Santa Cruz, she holds an M.F.A. from UMass Amherst and lives in Los Angeles.

Michael C Ford has recorded 81 spoken word tracks on vinyl, CD and laser disk formats. Since 1970 a wide range of indie presses have published approximately 28 volumes of print documents.

"Marie Windsor" was previously published in the following: *Ladies Above Suspicion* (book-length poetry from Illuminati, 1987) ; *Motel Café* (12-inch LP Vinyl disc from Blue Yonder Sounds Records & Tapes, 1988); Manteca Bulletin (North Central Valley tabloid, 1989); *Women Under The Influence* (Word Palace Press, 2015)

Sesshu Foster has taught composition and literature in East L.A. for more than 25 years. He's also taught writing at the University of Iowa, the California Institute for the Arts, the Jack Kerouac School for Disembodied Poetics Summer Writing Program and the University of California, Santa Cruz. His work has been published in *The Oxford Anthology of Modern American Poetry, Language for a New Century: Poetry from the Middle East, Asia and Beyond*, and *State of the Union: 50 Political Poems*.

"Time Studies #75" was originally published in The Poetry Loft (August, 2012). "Movie Version: Hell to Eternity" was originally published in Parrafo Magazine (#6).

Timothy Green has worked full-time for the last ten years as editor of the poetry journal Rattle. His book of poems, *American Fractal*, is available from Red Hen Press.

"Poem from Dark Matter" first appeared in Connecticut Review. "The Body" first appeared in Mid-American Review.

308

Amélie Frank is a Los Angeles native and the author of five poetry collections. Her work has appeared in numerous local, national, and international journals. She cofounded The Sacred Beverage Press and has served on the boards of the Valley Contemporary Poets and Beyond Baroque. Her biography appears in both *Who's Who in America* and *Who's Who of American Women*.

"It Came to Pass in a Backyard in Silver Lake" was printed in the catalog for the gallery exhibit of Matthew Mars' "Written on the World: 21st Century Cartography" and appeared in print on the wall as part of the exhibit (January, 2014).

Dr. Kate Gale is Managing Editor of Red Hen Press. She teaches in the MFA program at San Diego State University. She is author of five books of poetry and six librettos. Gale recently published two books: *The Goldilocks Zone*, (University of New Mexico Press) and *Echo Light* (Red Mountain Press).

Lucia Galloway was born in the agricultural Midwest, but has lived most of her life in California, the past 45 years in the Los Angeles area. Author of *Venus and Other Losses* (Plain View) and a chapbook, *Playing Outside* (Finishing Line), she also has poems in journals and anthologies. Lucia hosts the "Fourth Sundays" reading series at the Claremont Library.

"One Harvest" appeared online in draft form as a feature of Tupelo Press's 30/30 Project in 2014.

Jerry Garcia is a poet, photographer and filmmaker from Los Angeles. In 2006 he was chosen to participate in the Newer Poets XI Series by the L.A. Poetry Festival. He has been a co-director of the Valley Contemporary Poets and served as a member of Beyond Baroque's Board of Trustees.

Dana Gioia is a poet, critic, and teacher. Born in Los Angeles of Italian and Mexican ancestry, he attended Stanford and Harvard. He is currently the Judge Widney Professor of Poetry and Public Culture at the University of Southern California. He has published four collections of poetry, *Daily Horoscope* (1986), *The Gods of Winter* (1991), *Interrogations at Noon* (2001), which won the American Book Award, and *Pity the Beautiful* (2012); and three critical volumes, including *Can Poetry Matter?* (1992), an influential study of poetry's place in contemporary America.

The four poems included here are reprinted by permission of Graywolf Press: "Cruising with the Beach Boys" and "The Letter" are from *Daily Horoscope*. "Money" and "Planting a Sequoia" are from *The Gods of Winter*.

Steve Goldman has published in several journals. He has a collection of poetry, *The Canon of the Lone Ranger: A Hymn in Dysfunction*. He was the founder/MC of two alternative reading series' in Venice, CA. He is the founding director of The Beyond Baroque Experimental Theater of Poetry, (BOXTOP) and the MC of monthly readings there. He sings in choruses and teaches fencing.

"The Lone Ranger Goes to War" is from *The Canon of the Lone Ranger* (MorMun Press, L.A., 2012, 2nd edition), and was first published by Sybaritic Press, (LA) 2005.

liz gonzález, a fourth generation So Cali girl, grew up in San Bernardino and Rialto. Her poetry, fiction, and memoirs have appeared in numerous journals, periodicals, and anthologies. Currently, she teaches creative writing at community centers and through the UCLA Extension Writers' Program. Her most recent award includes an Irvine Fellowship in the Sally and Don Lucas Artists Residency Program at Montalvo Arts Center in Saratoga, California.

"The Four Food Groups in Grandma's Summer Lunches" was previously published in *Poetry in the Window VI*. "Espiritu" was published in Heliotrope, Winter 2004, and Strongbox.bizland.com. "Confessions of a Pseudo Chicana" was previously published in Speechless the Magazine, City of Los Angeles Latino Heritage Month Celebration 2007 Calendar and Cultural Guide, and Luna: A Journal of Poetry and Translation (Spring, 1999).

Jessica Goodheart's work has appeared in *The Best American Poetry* series, The Antioch Review, Pearl, Spillway and other journals. Her book, entitled *Earthquake Season,* was published by Word Press in 2010. Her poetry was featured four times in the Poetry in the Windows exhibit, sponsored by the Arroyo Arts Collective in Los Angeles. She works at a Los Angeles non-profit.

"Let Go" originally appeared in *Pearl.*

S.A. Griffin lives, loves and works in Los Angeles.

"I Choose Not to Believe in War Holy or Not" first published on a billboard during August 2002 at the corner of Sunset Blvd., Hollywood Blvd. and Hillhurst Ave. in Los Angeles. It has also appeared in *Duckwalking Thru the Apocalypse* (Bottle of Smoke, 2003), *Armageddon Outta Here!* (Rose of Sharon, 2004), *Numbskull Sutra* (Rank Stranger, 2007) and *Greatest Hits* (Pudding House, 2008).

Peter J. Harris is the author of *Bless the Ashes* (Tia Chucha Press) and *The Black Man of Happiness: In Pursuit of My 'Unalienable Right,'* a book of personal essays.

310

David Hernandez received the Kathryn A. Morton Prize for *Hoodwinked* (Sarabande Books, 2011). His awards include an NEA Literature Fellowship in Poetry and a Pushcart Prize. His poems have appeared in FIELD, The Southern Review, Ploughshares, and *The Best American Poetry 2013*. David teaches creative writing at California State University, Long Beach and is married to writer Lisa Glatt.

"Dear Professor" was previously published in Zyzzyva; "Against Erosion" in *Hoodwinked* (Sarabande Books, 2011); "Huntington Botanical Gardens" in *A House Waiting for Music* and "Planting the Palms" were previously published in *A House Waiting for Music* (Tupelo Press, 2003)

Bill Hickok began writing humor as a defense against his children's tyranny. He is the author of *The Woman Who Shot Me & Other Poems* (Whirlybird Press). His articles and poems have appeared on the Op-Ed pages of Cleveland Plain Dealer, Kansas City Star, Newsday, Philadelphia Enquirer, and in magazines, including *Uncle* (for those who have given up), and online. Bill passed away in 2014.

"Mahler & Me" first appeared in The Kansas City Star. "How to Get to Heaven" first appeared in *The Woman Who Shot Me*.

Jen Hofer is a poet, translator, social justice interpreter, teacher, knitter, book-maker, public letter-writer, urban cyclist, and co-founder of the language justice and language experimentation collaborative Antena and the local collective Antena Los Angeles. She publishes poems, translations, and visual-textual works with numerous small presses, including Action Books, Atelos, belladonna, Counterpath Press, Kenning Editions, Insert Press, Les Figues Press, and Litmus Press.

Eric Howard is a magazine editor who lives in Los Angeles. His poems have appeared in Birmingham Poetry Review, Caveat Lector, Conduit, Gulf Stream Magazine, Plainsong, and The Sun.

"To the Terrace House" was published previously in Crony.

Nan Hunt has been an educator in the Los Angeles area since 1972 and published widely in the U.S., Canada, India, Japan, England, and Ireland. She won grants and poetry awards from University of Florida, Suffield Conference (Louis Untermeyer), National Writers Union, Nimrod, Harcourt Brace (University of Colorado), Centrum, Ucross Foundation, and first place in poetry at the Jackson Arts Festival. She founded the long-running Valley Contemporary Poetry Series.

"Wilderness Pond at Dusk" was published previously in a volume of poetry by Nan Hunt entitled *The Wrong Bride* (Plain View Press).

Charlotte Innes has two chapbooks from Finishing Line Press, *Licking the Serpent* (2011) and *Reading Ruskin in Los Angeles* (2009). Her poetry has appeared in *The Best American Spiritual Writing 2006* (Houghton Mifflin), The Hudson Review, The Sewanee Review, The Raintown Review, and Rattle. She has written about books and the arts for the Los Angeles Times and The Nation. She has taught English, creative writing and journalism at high schools and colleges in and around Los Angeles.

"The Ex" originally appeared in R*attle* #40 (Summer, 2013).

Lois P. Jones is a host of Pacifica Radio's "Poet's Café," co-producer of the Moonday reading series and poetry editor of Kyoto Journal. Publications include Narrative Magazine, The Warwick Review, American Poetry Journal, Tupelo Quarterly, Texas Review Press (Sam Houston State University) and Eyewear (UK) She is the winner of the 2012 Tiferet and the 2012 Liakoura poetry prizes.

Eloise Klein Healy lives in Los Angeles with Colleen Rooney and their dog, Nikita. *A Wild Surmise: New and Selected Poems and Recordings*, which previously published the poems here, is her seventh book. She is the first Poet Laureate of Los Angeles.

"My Love Wants to Park" was originally published in *A Packet Beating Like a Heart*, 1981 and reprinted in *A Wild Surmise: New and Selected Poems and Recordings.* "Artemis in Echo Park" was originally published in *Artemis in Echo Park*, 1991 and reprinted in *A Wild Surmise.* "Dark" was originally published in *A Packet Beating Like a Heart*, 1981 and reprinted in *A Wild Surmise.*

Douglas Kearney is a Poet/performer/librettist whose third poetry collection, *Patter* (Red Hen Press) examines miscarriage, infertility, and parenthood. His second collection, *The Black Automaton,* was Catherine Wagner's selection for the National Poetry Series. Raised in Altadena, CA, he lives with his family in California's Santa Clarita Valley. He teaches at CalArts, where he received his MFA in Writing (2004).

"City of Searchlights and Dead Cats" is reprinted with permission from *The Black Automaton* (Fence Books, 2009).

Doug Knott is a poet, writer, performer, videographer, and raconteur. A member of troupes "The Lost Tribe" and "The Carma Bums," his recent work, "The Last of the Knotts," blends these modes in a theatrical performance, and has been staged in New York, LA, Florida, Mexico and Canada. He has been board president of Beyond Baroque Literary Arts Foundation since 2013.

Ron Koertge writes poetry for everyone and fiction for young adults. A prolific author, he has published more than twenty volumes of poetry and prose. His latest book of poems is *The Ogre's Wife* (Red Hen Press), while the most recent publication for teenage readers is *Coaltown Jesus* (Candlewick Press). A serious handicapper of thoroughbred horses, he can be found near the paddock at Santa Anita Race Track.

"Coloring" was collected in *Making Love to Roget's Wife* (U. of Arkansas Press, 1997) and "Little, Small, Wee Bear" appeared in The Horn Book Magazine.

Robin Coste Lewis is a Provost's Fellow in Poetry and Visual Studies at USC. A Cave Canem fellow, she received her MFA from NYU, and an MTS in Sanskrit from Harvard's Divinity School. A finalist for the International War Poetry Prize, the National Rita Dove Prize, and the Discovery Prize, her work has appeared in various journals and anthologies. She has taught at Wheaton College, Hunter College, Hampshire College and the NYU/MFA in Paris. Born in Compton, her family is from New Orleans. Her book of poems, *Voyage of the Sable Venus*, is forthcoming from Knopf.

"Frame" first appeared in Transition, "Body in August" in Phantom Limb.

Gerald Locklin is Professor Emeritus of English, California State University, Long Beach. His Books from 2013 include *Deep Meanings* (Presa Press), three novellas (Spout Hill Press), and *Le Dernier des Damnes* (13 eNote Editions, Paris). He is archived by the CSULB Library Special Collections and is the subject of *A Critical Introduction to Gerald Locklin,* edited by Michael Basinski.

"Green Corn Tamales" was published in *The Life Force Poems*, Water Row Press: Sudbury, MA, copyright © Gerald Locklin, 2002, by permission of the author. "I've Always Enjoyed Her Sense of Humor" was published in Gerald Locklin: *New and Selected Poems*, edited by Paul Kareem Tayyar, Silver Birch Press: Los Angeles, CA, copyright © Gerald Locklin 2013, by permission of the author.

Suzanne Lummis studied poetry at CSU Fresno, and has been a longtime teacher for the UCLA Extension Writers' Program. *Open 24 Hours* received the Blue Lynx Poetry Prize, and she's had poems in The New Yorker, The Antioch Review, Ploughshares, Hotel Amerika. Together with her students she wrote, *The Poetry Mystique: Inside the Contemporary Poetry Workshop* (2015). She's the 2015 recipient of Beyond Baroque's GDS Outstanding Achievement in Poetry Award. And she's one of the Nearly Fatal Women.

"Street Dumb" was in The Hudson Review, "Gone, Baby" in Connotationpress.com and later in *New California Poets, 2012* (Heyday Books).

Rick Lupert has been involved with L.A. poetry since 1990. He received Beyond Baroque's 2014 Distinguished Service Award and created the Poetry Super Highway site. He's hosted the Cobalt Cafe reading since 1994 and has authored 16 collections including *The Gettysburg Undress*, and edited the anthologies *Ekphrastia Gone Wild*, *A Poet's Haggadah* and *The Night Goes on All Night*.

The poems "Homesick" and "The Cheese King" originally appeared in the book *Death of a Mauve Bat* (Ain't Got No Press, 2012).

Sarah Maclay is the author of *Music for the Black Room, The White Bride*, and *Whore* (U. of Tampa Press). Her poems, criticism, and theatre pieces have appeared in APR, Ploughshares, FIELD, The Writer's Chronicle, *The Best American Erotic Poems: from 1800 to the Present*, *Scenarios: Scripts to Perform*, Poetry International, and elsewhere. The recipient of the Tampa Review Prize for Poetry, she teaches creative writing and literature at Loyola Marymount University and conducts workshops at Beyond Baroque.

The poem "as, after Odysseus, her body wanted to be Ophelia" first appeared in The Superstition Review. "Grille," from *The White Bride* (U of Tampa Press), was first published in FIELD.

Holaday Mason's books include *Light Spilling From Its Own Cup* (Inevitable Press,1999), *Towards the Forest* and *Dissolve* (New River Press, 2011). Her manuscripts *Her Body Became a Medium*, co-written with Sarah Maclay, and *The Weaver's Body* (finalist and honorable mention for the 2013 Dorset Prize) are seeking publication. Her poems have been published in Poetry International, American Literary Review, Pool, Smartish Pace, and Runes.

Robert Mezey has edited ten books, including *Poems of the American West* (Knopf, Everyman Series), *Thomas Hardy: Selected Poems* (Penguin Classics), and *A Word Like Fire: The Selected Poems of Dick Barnes*. With Stephen Berg he edited the groundbreaking 1960s anthology, *Naked Poetry*. He received the Robert Frost Prize (at Kenyon), the Lamont Prize for his poetry collection *The Lovemaker*, a PEN prize and a Bassine Citation for *Evening Wind* (Wesleyan). Born in Philadelphia, he became first in his family to go to college, or even high school.

"Please?" won the Ann Silver Award and was published in Speechlessthemagazine.org, "Beau Jack," in Friscoboxing.com.

William Mohr is an associate professor at California State University, Long Beach, where he teaches twentieth century American literature and is a core member of the MFA faculty. In addition to several collections of poetry, he is the author of a literary history of Los Angeles poetry, *Holdouts: The Los Angeles Poetry Renaissance 1948-1992* (University of Iowa Press, 2011). He was the 2014 recipient of Beyond Baroque's George Drury Smith Award.

"One Miracle" appeared in Wormwood Review (vol. 36, number 2; issue 142), and was subsequently translated into Spanish by José Luis Rico and appeared as "Un Milagro" in *Circulo de Poesia: Revista Electronica de Literatura* (circulodepoesia.com, 2012). "In Line at Pancho's Tacos" appeared in Barney: The Modern Stone Age Magazine (1982) and was reprinted in *Hidden Proofs* (Bombshelter Press, 1982); "Big Band, Slow Dance" appeared in Santa Monica Review (1996), and was reprinted in *Bittersweet Kaleidoscope* (IF/SF Editions, 2006).

Henry J. Morro, founding editor of the Pacific Coast Poetry Series, an imprint of Beyond Baroque Books, is the author of the poetry collection *Corpses of Angels* (Bombshelter Press). His poetry has been published in numerous journals—including Seneca Review, New Letters, Black Warrior Review, Poet Lore, ASKEW, Chiron Review, California Quarterly, Sonora Review, Pacific Review, and in *The Outlaw Bible of American Poetry* (Thunder's Mouth Press).

"Any Job" was published in Sonora Review; "Three Generations of Loving Marilyn" was published in Malpais Review; and "The Boxing Shrine" was published in Poet Lore.

Carol Muske-Dukes is former Poet Laureate of California, author of 8 books of poems, 4 novels, 2 essay collections and has co-edited anthologies. Her books have received numerous awards, including a National Book Award nomination, L.A.Times Book Prize nomination, New York Times Most Notable Books, Castognola Award from the Poetry Society of America, Barnes & Noble Writer for Writers award, Guggenheim, NEA, plus 6 Pushcart Prizes. She is Professor of English/Creative Writing at USC, where she founded the PhD program in Creative Writing/Literature.

"Condolence Note" was previously published in The Paris Review; "Twin Tree" appears in Smartish Pace, Issue 17, and then on Poetry Daily; "After Skate" on Academy of American Poets' Poem-a-Day website.

Majid Naficy, the Arthur Rimbaud of Persian poetry, fled Iran in 1983, a year and a half after the execution of his wife Ezzat in Tehran. Since 1984 he has been living in West Los Angeles. Majid's books include *Muddy*

Shoes (Beyond Baroque Books, 1999), and *Father and Son* (Red Hen Press, 2003) as well as his doctoral dissertation at UCLA "Modernism and Ideology in Persian Literature" (University Press of America, 1997). His poetry is in public spaces in Venice Beach and Studio City.

"Chess" and "Hope" were previously posted on Iranian.com and Iroon.com websites.

Harry E. Northup has had ten poetry books published, including *Where Bodies Again Recline.* Harry was an original member of the Wednesday night poetry workshop that began in early 1969 at Beyond Baroque. Northup received his B.A. in English, at CSUN, where he studied verse with Ann Stanford. He is a founding member of Cahuenga Press and is married to the poet Holly Prado.

The poems "Make a Poem" and "Both Ways on Prospect" were first posted on Times Times 3.

Wendy C. Ortiz is the author of *Excavation: A Memoir* (Future Tense Books). She has written a year-long column for McSweeney's Internet Tendency, and her work has appeared in The New York Times, Vol. 1 Brooklyn, The Nervous Breakdown and The Rumpus, among many other journals.

"Some Scars" originally appeared in Blood Orange Review. "Accused 1 & 2" originally appeared in Finery, an online journal from Birds of Lace. "The Women in My Family" originally appeared on womenwriters.net.

Judith Pacht's *Summer Hunger* (Tebot Bach) won the 2011 PEN Southwest Book Award for Poetry. She's had poems in Ploughshares, Runes, Phoebe, Nimrod and, translated into English, Foreign Literature (Moscow, Russia). Her poem "Undelivered Mothers' Day" took first place in the Georgia Poetry Society's Edgar Bowers competition, and her poems appear in numerous anthologies. Her chapbook, also her first poetry collection, *Falcon* (Conflux Press), was published in 2004.

"*Bird*" appeared in the Cider Press Review and in *Summer Hunger.*

Sherman Pearl, a retired journalist, is immediate past president of Beyond Baroque and a former director of Valley Contemporary Poets. He also served on the founding committee of the Los Angeles Poetry Festival. His work has appeared in more than 50 literary journals and anthologies and has won awards from the National Writers Union and the Strokestown (Ireland) Poetry Festival, among others.

"What I Came For" was published in Poetry Flash and "Salvation in the Dead Zone" in Margie Poetry Journal.

316

Candace Pearson's *Hour of Unfolding* won the 2010 Liam Rector First Book Prize for Poetry from Briery Creek Press, Longwood University. She has poems in fine journals nationwide and in several anthologies, including *Beyond Forgetting: Poetry and Prose about Alzheimer's Disease* and *Sharing the Seasons: A Book of Poems*. She lives in the Los Angeles hills.

"The Neurologist" was previously published in The Cimarron Review

Cece Peri's poems have appeared in Malpais Review, Luvina, Speechless, NoirCon, and Capital & Main. She was selected as an ALOUD Newer Poet, received the first Anne Silver Poetry Award, a Pushcart Prize nomination, and awards from NoirCon 2012, and Arroyo Arts Collective's 2014 Poetry in the Windows. A New Yorker, she has lived in Los Angeles since 2003.

"Trouble Down the Road" appeared in Luvina (December 2009 under the title, "The Fry Cook"), and in Malpais Review *(*Winter 2012-2013), and The Arroyo Arts Collective Poetry in the Windows (2014). "The White Chicken Gives a First-Hand Account" appeared in Writers at Work's *Poem of the Month,* September 2009. "It's Noir" appeared in *NoirCon 2012* (Busted Flush Press).

Alice Pero's book of poetry, *Thawed Stars*, was hailed by Kenneth Koch as having "clarity and surprises." Pero has taught poetry to grade school children in private and public schools for 23 years. Her work can be found in many journals throughout the U.S. In 2002 she founded the reading series, "Moonday" in Los Angeles. Pero is an accomplished flutist.

"Directions for Eating a Mountain" appeared in di-vêrsé-city as "Mountain Meal."

Dennis Phillips is the author of more than a dozen books of poetry, including *Measures* (Talisman, 2013), and *Navigation: Selected Poems, 1985 – 2010* (Otis Books/Seismicity Editions, 2011). In 1998 he edited and wrote the introduction for a book of the early essays of James Joyce, *Joyce on Ibsen (*Green Integer). His novel, *Hope* (Green Integer) came out in 2007.

The poems "On Exile" and "On Zygotes and Thanatos" appear in the book *Measures* (Talisman House Publishers, 2013). Both poems were previously published individually in the journal OR.

Holly Prado's eleventh book, *Oh, Salt/Oh, Desiring Hand,* was published in Fall, 2013 by Cahuenga Press. She's been an active part of the Los Angeles poetry community since the early 1970s.

"Earning a Living" published in *Oh, Salt/ Oh, Desiring Hand,* (Cahuenga Press, 2013).

James Ragan has authored 8 books of poetry and two plays. Translated into 12 languages, he has read for six heads of state with honors including three Fulbright Professorships, two Honorary Doctorates, the Emerson Poetry Prize, 8 Pushcart Prize nominations, a PSA Citation, and the Swan Foundation Humanitarian Award, among others. He is the subject of the documentary "Flowers and Roots." (Arina Films, 2014).

"Shouldering the World" appears in the book *The World Shouldering I* (Salmon Publishers, Ireland, 2013); "Rilke on the Conveyor Belt at Los Angeles International" is from *Lusions* (Grove/Atlantic, N.Y., 1997)

Ellen Reich teaches creative writing and autobiography for Santa Monica College. Her poems have most recently been published in Third Wednesday, Slant, Common Ground, If & When, Rockhurst Review, Earth's Daughters, Bryant Literary Review. Her fifth poetry book is forthcoming from Tebot Bach, entitled *Sacrifices Have to Be Human*.

"Tree, You Took Too Long to Bloom" was previously published in Poetry/LA.

Marilyn N. Robertson has been a participant in the Summer Poetry in Idyllwild, a featured reader in Viva Poetry, and in The Los Angeles Poetry Festival's 2011 series of events Night and the City: L.A. Noir in Poetry, Fiction and Film, coordinated by Suzanne Lummis. She has a poem in the on-line magazines Speechlessthemagazine.org, The Boston Literary Magazine and Capitol and Main. One of her poems was featured in the public arts project, Poetry and the Windows, on Figueroa in NELA.

"How to Eat a California Orange" was chosen as the November 2010, Poem of the Month by Writers at Work, coordinated by Terry Wolverton.

Luis J. Rodriguez is current Poet Laureate of Los Angeles. His latest poetry book is *My Nature is Hunger: New & Selected Poems*. Luis has read in Los Angeles, San Francisco, San Diego, Chicago, Seattle, Miami, New Orleans, Toronto, Montreal, Guadalajara, Caracas, Buenos Aires, Mexico City, San Salvador, Guatemala City, London, Heidelberg, and Berlin. He is founder/editor of Tia Chucha Press and co-founder of Tia Chucha's Centro Cultural & Bookstore in the San Fernando Valley.

"The Monster" and "Palmas" first appeared in the poetry collection *Poems Across the Pavement* (Tia Chucha Press, 1989) and reprinted in a 25th year anniversary edition in 2014. Both poems were in *Slam Poetry: Heftige Dichtung Aus Amerika* (German translations of American poets) (Druckhaus Galrev, 1993). "Palmas" was featured in *A Snake in the Heart: Poems & Music by Chicago's Spoken Word Performers*, a recording in 1994 by Tia Chucha Press, Chicago. "The Monster" was also in *Opening Doors: English as a Second Language Workbook* (Main Street Rag Publishing, 2002); *Dream of a Word: The Tia Chucha Press Poetry Anthology* (Tia Chucha Press, 2005); *Cool Salsa: Bilingual*

Poems on Growing up Latino in the United States (Henry Holt & CO. 1994); and the Los Angeles Times, October 16, 2005.

Melissa Roxas is a poet, health worker, and human rights activist. She has been active in community and social justice work for over eighteen years. Melissa is a survivor of abduction and torture by the Philippine military. A Kundiman, PEN USA Emerging Voices, and Great Leap Collaboratory fellow, her work has been published in Rhino, Boxcar Poetry, and Solo Novo. She studied poetry in the UCLA Extension Writers' Program.

"Geography Lesson" first appeared in Boxcar Poetry Review.

Mehnaz Sahibzada was born in Pakistan and lives in Los Angeles. She is a 2009 PEN USA Emerging Voices Fellow in Poetry. Her short story, "The Alphabet Workbook," appeared in the August 2010 issue of Ellery Queen Mystery Magazine. She has a poetry chapbook, *Tongue-Tied: A Memoir in Poems* (Finishing Line Press, 2012). "Damsel Ghost" was written in a response to an image writing workshop led by Tresha Haefner.

"Muse Noir" was published in The Five-Two: Crime Poetry Weekly (June 2014).

Cathie Sandstrom's work has appeared in Ploughshares, Runes, Lyric, Solo, Comstock Review, Cider Press Review, Malpais Review, ART/LIFE, Periphery, New Plains Review and Presence. Anthologies include *Open Windows, Blue Arc West, So Luminous the Wildflowers* and *Matchbook*. Her poem "You Again," is in the artists' book collections at the Getty Museum, Los Angeles, and the University of Southern California.

"Releasing the Birds" was published in *Open Windows* by the Arroyo Arts Collective (2005).

Patty Seyburn has published four books of poems: *Hilarity* (New Issues Press, 2009), *Mechanical Cluster* (Ohio State University Press, 2002) and *Diasporadic* (Helicon Nine Editions, 1998), and her most recent, *Perfecta* (What Books Press, 2014). She is an Associate Professor at California State University, Long Beach and co-editor of POOL: A Journal of Poetry.

"November" was published in Corridors Magazine, 2011; "Long Distance" in Women in Judaism, 2007; "What I Disliked about the Pleistocene Era" in Poetry, October 2005.

Mike Sonksen, aka Mike the Poet, is a 3rd-generation Angeleno. His first book — *I Am Alive In Los Angeles!* is in the curriculum of over 60 universities and high schools. In 2013, the Beyond Baroque Literary Arts Center awarded Mike for "Distinguished Service to the Los Angeles Poetry Community." His KCET column "LA Letters" celebrates bright moments from literary Los Angeles and beyond.

"The Arroyo Seco" is published in the book *I Am Alive in Los Angeles Remixed* (Writ Large Press, Fall 2014).

David St. John is the author of eleven collections of poetry (including *Study for the World's Body*, nominated for The National Book Award), and most recently, *The Auroras* and *The Window*. He is also the co-editor of *American Hybrid: A Norton Anthology of New Poetry*. He teaches in the Ph.D. Program in Literature and Creative Writing at The University of Southern California and lives in Venice Beach.

Sections VIII and XIX were first published in *The Face: A Novella in Verse* (HarperCollins, 2004); reprinted by permission of HarperCollins and David St. John. "Gin" first appeared in the collection, *Hush* (1976); © 2014, David St. John; reprinted by permission of the author. "Night" first appeared in *The Red Leaves of Night* (1999); © 2014, David St. John; reprinted by permission of the author.

Timothy Steele's books of poems include *The Color Wheel* and *Toward the Winter Solstice*. He has also published a pair of widely discussed books of literary criticism, *Missing Measures* and *All the Fun's in How You Say a Thing*. He is an emeritus professor of English at California State University, Los Angeles.

"Toward the Winter Solstice" from *Toward the Winter Solstice*, Copyright © 2006 by Timothy Steele. Used by permission of Swallow Press/Ohio University Press. "Haydn in Los Angeles" has not yet been collected in a book, so the author still holds reprint rights. (The poem first "appeared" on the May 4, 2013 edition of KUSC's Arts Alive, when it was broadcast as one of the winners in a poetry contest the station had held in the previous month in connection with National Poetry Month.)

Austin Straus is a painter, retired English instructor, and performer of his poetry. He frequently, informally, exhibits prints, one-of-a-kind artists' books, and paintings in conjunction with readings at libraries, community arts centers, galleries. The former Southwest Regional Coordinator of Amnesty International and Poetry Connexion radio talk-show host has published two books of poems with Red Hen Press: *Drunk with Light* (2002) and *Intensifications* (2010), for which he did the cover art. He was married to the late Wanda Coleman.

"If I Were a Wall" and "Even Paranoids..." are from *Intensifications* (Red Hen Press, 2010); "L.A. Morning" is from *Drunk with Light* (Red Hen, 2002).

Amber Tamblyn is an actress and poet who has been nominated for an Emmy, Golden Globe and Spirit Award for her work in television and film. She has published two collections of poetry and her third, *Dark Sparkler* (Harper Collins) will be released in Spring, 2015. It examines the lives and deaths of child star actresses.

Judith Taylor is the author of three poetry collections, *Sex Libris* (What Books Press), *Curios* (Sarabande Books), and *Selected Dreams from the Animal Kingdom* (Zoo Press). Formerly on the faculty of UCLA Extension Writers' Program, she now teaches privately. Taylor is one of the founding editors of POOL: A Journal of Poetry and has managed and co-edited the journal since its inception in 2002.

"Black Pot" and "The Well-Stocked Home" were previously published in *Sex Libris* (What Books Press, 2013). "How Am I Driving?" is from the book *Selected Dreams from the Animal Kingdom* (Zoo Press, 2003).

Judith Terzi arrived at Union Station from Philadelphia the summer before sixth grade and had to quickly learn how to pronounce Tujunga and La Cienega. She holds an M.A. in French Lit and taught high school French for many years as well as English at California State University, Los Angeles, and in Algiers, Algeria. Her poetry appears in many journals and anthologies.

"L.A. Retro-Specs" was previously published in South85, 2012.

Lynne Thompson has authored two chapbooks, *We Arrive by Accumulation* and *Through a Window*. Her first full-length manuscript, *Beg No Pardon,* won the Perugia Press Book Award and the Great Lakes Colleges Association's New Writers Award. Her latest manuscript, *Start With a Small Guitar,* was published by What Books Press in October, 2013.

"Song for Two Immigrants" was previously published in Crab Orchard Review.

Mary Torregrossa is an ESL teacher in the San Gabriel Valley area. In 2014, the Arroyo Arts Collective awarded Mary a first prize in "Poetry in the Windows." "Signs" was published in Juan Felipe Herrera's *Poems for Unity.* Mary was chosen for the Writers' Club of Whittier, 2013 Poetry Prize and in 2009 was selected by the Los Angeles Poetry Festival for the prestigious Newer Poets event, part of the ALOUD series at The Los Angeles Public Library - downtown. She has been published on-line in poeticdiversity, Writers at Work and the East Jazmine Review.

Mitchell Untch was a 2011 finalist for The Atlantic Review International, a finalist for the 2012 C.P. Cavafy Award; Ruminate Magazine Finalist; a Semi-finalist for the Puamantock 2012 Poetry Prize. Publications include: Confrontation; Nimrod Intl; upstreet; The Beloit Poetry Journal; South Dakota Review; Solo Novo; Natural Bridge; Southern Humanities; The Fourth River; The Hawaii Review; Kestrel; Ruminate Magazine; Out of Ours; Poet Lore (2013) and North American Review.

"Estate Sale" appeared in North American Review, Fall 2013. "Sycamore" in Jabberwock Review, Summer 2011; "Dear Betty Blythe Francis" in Poet Lore, Fall/Winter 2013; and "Coming Out (Mother/Father)" in Upstreet, Number 8

Amy Uyematsu is a sansei poet from Los Angeles. Her publications include three collections, *30 Miles from J-Town, Nights of Fire, Nights of Rain*, and *Stone Bow Prayer*, as well as a fourth book, *The Yellow Door*, due out in 2015. Now retired, Amy worked as a high school math teacher for over three decades.

"The Accusation" was previously published by Bamboo Ridge Journal in 2012. "Kickball" was previously published by ASKEW in 2011.

Gloria Vando's books and poems have won the Poetry Society of America's Di Castagnola Award and Latino Literary Hall of Fame's Poetry Book Award. Her most recent book, *Woven Voices: 3 Generations of Puertorriqueña Poets Look at Their American Lives* (Scapegoat Press, 2012) is a compilation of poems by Anita Velez-Mitchell, Anika Paris, and herself. Gloria is publisher/editor of Helicon Nine Editions (recipient of the Kansas Governor's Arts Award) and co-founder of The Writers Place.

"My 90-Year-Old Father and My Husband Discuss Their Trips to the Moon" appeared in New Letters *(*2010). Both poems were included in *Woven Voices: 3 Generations of Puertorriqueña Poets Look at Their American Lives* (Anita Velez-Mitchell, Gloria Vando, Anika Paris; Scapegoat Press, 2012). "He2-104: A True Planetary Nebula in the Making" won first prize in the Billee Murray Denny Poetry Award contest.

Paul Vangelisti has published more than 20 books of poetry and is a noted translator from Italian. His most recent book of poems, *Two*, appeared in 2011, while a memoir of sorts, *Wholly Falsetto with People Dancing*, followed in 2013. Also, in 2010, his translation of Adriano Spatola's *The Position of Things: Collected Poems, 1961-1992*, won the Academy of American Poets translation book prize. He is Founding Chair of the Graduate Writing program at Otis College of Art and Design.

The poem "Alephs Again" was first published in book form in 1999, in the collection *Alphabets* (Los Angeles: Littoral Books).

Rolland Vasin: Vachine is a pseudonym for a performance poet and CPA named Rolland Vasin who reads at open mics from coast to coast in the USA, has been featured at leading Los Angeles literary venues and was recognized at LA's Laugh Factory as the 3rd funniest CPA in Los Angeles. When he's not writing poetry, or auditing charities, he resides in Santa Monica, California where he bodysurfs, plays banjo, and guitar, but not all at the same time.

Sharon Venezio is the author of *The Silence of Doorways* (Moon Tide Press, 2013). Her poems have appeared in Spillway, Bellevue Literary Review, Midway Journal, Reed, and elsewhere. She lives in Los Angeles where she works as a behavior analyst specializing in Autism.

"College Essay" appeared in Lily Literary Review, February 2012; "Psychology 402: Brain and Behavior" in Chaparral, July 2012.

Antonieta Villamil brings a cross-cultural experience to her poetry with a mixture of stanzas using voice and deep song. The result is an alchemical fusion of rhythms and voices from the Middle-East, India, Spain, Africa, to the Latino African, and indigenous peoples of America. She focuses on the forgotten ones and honors them with a persistence that compels us to hear their voices. Antonieta Villamil won the "14th International Latino Book Award, 2012" with Soluna En Bosque for Best Book of Poetry in The United States. She appears next to Emily Dickinson, Walt Whitman, Langston Hughes among others in the documentary "Voices In Wartime." Antonieta's brother, Pedro, "died of disappearance" in 1990. He is among a long list of people that disappear every day in Central and South American Countries. The poem "Memory of Moss" is a gravestone to his memory.

Charles Harper Webb's latest book, *What Things Are Made Of*, was published by the University of Pittsburgh Press in 2013. Recipient of grants from the Whiting and Guggenheim foundations, and Editor of *Stand Up Poetry: An Expanded Anthology*, Webb teaches in the MFA Program in Creative Writing at California State University, Long Beach.

"Marilyn's Machine," from *Reading the Water*, published by Northeastern University Press, © 1997 by Charles Harper Webb. Reprinted by permission of the author. "Wedding Dress" from *Liver*, published by The University of Wisconsin Press, © 1999 by The Board of Regents of the University of Wisconsin System. Reprinted by permission of the author. "Tenderness in Men" from *Liver*, published by The University of Wisconsin Press, © 1999 by The Board of Regents of the University of Wisconsin System. Reprinted by permission of the author. "Parasites," first published by Miramar. Reprinted by permission of the author.

Florence Weinberger is the author of four collections of poetry, *The Invisible Telling Its Shape, Breathing Like a Jew , Carnal Fragrance*, and *Sacred Graffiti*. Twice nominated for a Pushcart Prize, Florence has been anthologized and has appeared in numerous literary magazines, including The Comstock Review, Calyx, River Styx, Nimrod, Poetry East and Rattle. In 2012 she served as a judge for the PEN Center USA Literary Contest.

"The Light Gatherers" was previously published in the chapbook *Breathing Like a Jew* (Chickory Blue Press)

Hilda Weiss is the co-founder and artistic director of www.Poetry.LA, a website featuring videos of poets and poetry venues in Southern California. Her chapbook, "Optimism About Trees," was nominated for a Pushcart prize in 2011. Her poetry has been published in journals such as ASKEW, Ekphrasis, Poemeleon, Rattle, and Salamander, among others.

"Streetwise in LA" was previously published by Salamander.

Jackson Wheeler was born in 1952 in Andrews, NC where he grew up. He attended UNC-Chapel Hill from 1971-1975 and then moved to California. He ended up in Oxnard working for the Association for Retarded Citizens, now ARC. He published his first poem in 1972, in Cellar Door undergraduate literary magazine. His publications include *Swimming Past Iceland* (1993); *A Near Country: Poems of Loss*, with Glenna Luschei and David Oliveira (1999). Bruce's poems have appeared in a variety of literary journals, including LA Review, Shenandoah, Carolina Quarterly, Rattapallax, Prairie Schooner, ASKEW, Rivertalk, Kayak and Agenda.

"Ars Poetica" was first published in AGENDA the British literary journal in 1995, reprinted in ASKEW (Vol. one issue 2).

Rex Wilder's new volume, *Boomerangs in the Living Room*, was released by Red Hen Press in 2013. It presents a form he invented, a four-line poem in which the last word rhymes with the first and can be recited in a single breath. He is currently editing *There and Back, A Boomerang Anthology*, also a Red Hen imprint.

"Wasted)", "Blog)", and "Romance)" appeared in Harvard Review 45 (2014) and Harvard Review Online.

Bruce Williams taught writing at Mt. San Antonio College for many years. He is widely published including several chapbooks and his first full-length book *The Mojave Road and Other Journeys* was published in 2010. Bruce's next book, *Like a Relic or a Child* his forthcoming from Tebot Bach.

"Arrangement of Optimism" is in *Like a Relic or a Child*, forthcoming from Tebot Bach.

Conney Williams is a poet, actor, and performance artist. He has two collections of poetry *Leaves of Spilled Spirit from an Untamed Poet* (2002) and *Blues Red Soul Falsetto* (2012). He is the Artistic Director at the World Stage and Coordinator for the Anansi Writers Workshop.

Cecilia Woloch is an NEA fellowship recipient and the author of five collections of poems, most recently *Carpathia* (BOA Editions 2009). The founding director of Summer Poetry in Idyllwild, she has also served on the faculties of a number of graduate and undergraduate creative writing programs. She currently teaches independently throughout the U.S. and around the world.

"My Old True Love" first appeared in Roger: An Art & Literary Magazine (Vol. 1, 2006) and in *Narcissus* (Tupelo Press 2008) and in *Carpathia*, (BOA Editions, 2009). "East India Grill Villanelle" first appeared in Kalliope (Vol. XXII, No. 2, 2000) and was subsequently in *Late* (BOA Editions, 2003). "Why I Believed, as a Child, That People Had Sex in Bathrooms" first appeared in New Letters (Vol. 72, 2006) and subsequently in *Carpathia* (BOA Editions, 2009).

Sholeh Wolpé was born in Iran, and spent most of her teen years in Trinidad and the UK before settling in the United States. A recipient of the 2014 PEN/Heim Translation Fund award, 2013 Midwest Book Award and 2010 Lois Roth Persian Translation prize, Wolpé is the author of three collections of poetry and two books of translations, and is the editor of three anthologies. She lives in Los Angeles.

"How Hard Is It to Write a Love Song?" is from her book *Keeping Time With Blue Hyacinths* (University of Arkansas Press, 2013); "The Outsider" is from *Rooftops of Tehran* by (Red Hen Press, 2008).

Terry Wolverton is the author of ten books of poetry, fiction and creative nonfiction. She is the founder of Writers At Work, a creative writing studio in Los Angeles and is also Affiliate Faculty in the MFA Writing Program of Antioch University Los Angeles and an instructor of Kundalini Yoga.

"Paradox" was originally published in Prairie Schooner (Spring 2004, p. 84.).
"In Praise of Jokes" and "In Praise of Traffic on the 405" were originally
published in *Shadow and Praise (*Main Street Rag Publishing Company, 2007).
"Hopscotch Highway" was originally published on the blog disarticulations (May
14, 2013).

Gail Wronsky lives in Topanga, California, and is the author of ten books
of poetry, prose, and translations. Her poems have appeared in Poetry,
Pool, Volt, Denver Quarterly, Boston Review, and other literary
magazines. She is Director of Creative Writing at Loyola Marymount
University.

"Beneath the Ganges Where it is Dark" and "Go On, Sure, Why Not" were
originally published in Crazyhorse, and later included in the chapbook *Blue
Shadow Behind Everything Dazzling* (Hollyridge Press); "Clearer than amber
gliding over stones" was published by Teesta Rangeet in Sikkim, India.

Stephen Yenser is a poet, critic, and editor. He is the author of the poetry
collections *Stone Fruit* (forthcoming), *Blue Guide* (2006) and *The Fire in
All Things* (1993). A winner of the Walt Whitman Award of the Academy
of American Poets, he has also received an Ingram Merrill Foundation
Award in Poetry and the Bernard F. Connors Prize for Poetry from the
Paris Review. Yenser is Distinguished Professor and Director of Creative
Writing at UCLA.

"Paradise Cove" was originally published in the collection *Blue Guide* (U. of
Chicago Press, 2006)

Sung Yol Yi was born in Korea. After he came to the United States in
1976, he attended Cal-State University of LA and UCLA Extension,
where he studied English poetry with Suzanne Lummis. In 1987, his poem
"The Last Moon" appeared in the Los Angeles Times. In 2002 his poem
"The Stray Dogs" was published in Poetry International, and in 2003,
"The Belt" was awarded first prize for Poetry in the Window by the
Arroyo Arts Collective. In May 2008, his first poetry book *The Stray Dogs*
was published by Xlibris. Currently, he resides in Los Angeles, teaching,
writing, and translating poetry.

Mariano Zaro has published four bilingual poetry books: *Where
From/Desde Donde, Poems of Erosion/Poemas de la erosión, The House
of Mae Rim/La casa de Mae Rim* and *Tres letras/Three Letters*. His short
stories are included in several journals in Spain and United States. He has
translated American poets Philomene Long (*The California Mission
Poems*) and Tony Barnstone (*Buddha in Flames*).

*noted, permission rights have been granted by the poets